W9-AFE-572

FROM SEX OBJECTS

TO SEXUAL SUBJECTS

FROM SEX OBJECTS

TO SEXUAL SUBJECTS

Claudia Moscovici

ROUTLEDGE　　　　　NEW YORK AND LONDON

Published in 1996 by

Routledge
29 West 35th Street
New York, NY 10001

Published in Great Britain in 1996 by

Routledge
11 New Fetter Lane
London EC4P 4EE

© Routledge 1996

Printed in the United States of America on acid-free paper.

All rights reserved. No part of this book may be reprinted or reproduced
or utilized in any form or by any electronic, mechanical or other means,
now known or hereafter invented, including photocopying and record-
ing, or in any information storage or retrieval system, without permission
in writing from the publishers.

Library of Congress Cataloging-in-Publication Data

Moscovici, Claudia, 1969-
    From sex objects to sexual subjects / Claudia Moscovici
       p.   cm.
    Includes bibliographical references and index.
    ISBN 0-415-91810-3 (hb) -- ISBN 0-415-91811-1 (pb)
    1. Feminist theory 2. Sex differences 3. Subjectivity
    4. Gender identity I. Title.
HQ1190.M68 1996
305.42'01--dc20   96-30437
                                 CIP

Design and typesetting by Leslie Sharpe
with Hermann Feldhaus at Cave.

To my parents and to the memory of my grandparents

CONTENTS

ACKNOWLEDGEMENTS

I am very grateful for the encouragement and extremely helpful critiques offered by Neil Lazarus, who has read most of this work, and whose critical and ethical engagement with Marxian and feminist thought will always be a source of inspiration for me. I would also like to thank Ellen Rooney, whose seminar on sexual difference in the fall of 1993 enabled me to examine critically, rather than simply enthusiastically, the works of contemporary French and American feminist theorists, particularly those of Luce Irigaray. I am grateful to Professors Michel-André Bossy, Chair of the Department of Comparative Literature (Brown University), and Edward Ahearn, Professor of French Studies and Graduate Advisor of the Department of Comparative Literature (Brown University), for offering their help and support when graduate students needed it most.

The seminars and enriching professional discussions with Michelle Perrot, Geneviève Fraisse, Françoise Collin and Etienne Balibar motivated my reflections on the possible intersections between feminist, Marxian, and democratic theories, particularly concerning the issues of parity and proportional group representation. I am extremely grateful to all of them for their intellectual guidance and for welcoming me to their seminars at the Collège International de Philosophie and the École des Hautes Études en Sciences Sociales in 1994–95. Last but not least, this work might have never seen print had it not been for the interest and encouragement offered by Nancy Fraser and Linda Nicholson, as well as for the constant source of inspiration I find in their works. I would like to thank University Press of America for permission to reprint the essay "The Field of Cultural Production: A Second Glance at the Erotic, the Aesthetic, and the Social" in this collection.

I dedicate this book to the memory of my grandparents and to my parents. My grandparents, Surica and Avram Moscovici and Gina and Mitica Buzulica, who offered me a happy and unforgettable childhood despite difficult circumstances, will always live in my unwaning affection for them. I am immensely indebted to my parents, Elvira Buzulica Moscovici and Henri Moscovici, for constantly encouraging my intellectual endeavors and ethical commitments and, above all, for being the most caring, sensitive and loving parents I could possibly imagine or desire. Danut Troyka lives out my egalitarian vision of a fair, generous and understanding spouse. His intelligent discussions and critiques of my thought and work, honed by his excellent training in law, extend my horizons beyond academic institutions and make me constantly reflect upon the implications and effects of academic critiques upon the different kinds of institutions that some people refer to as "the real world."

INTRODUCTION

Any theory of the "subject" will have been appropriated to the "masculine." Subjecting herself to it, woman would be unwittingly renouncing the specificity of any relationship to the imaginary—either by putting herself back in the position of being objectified—as "feminine"—by discourse, or by reobjectifying herself when she claims to identify with it "as" a masculine subject. . . . Subjectivity denied to woman is, without any doubt, the collateral for any irreducible constitution of object: representation, discourse, or desire. Imagine that woman imagines—the ob-ject would therein lose its fixed character of an "idea." . . . If the earth turned, especially if it turned about itself, the erection of the subject might risk becoming disconcerted both in its elevation and in its momentum. For what would it arise from and upon what could it exercise its power? Or in what? The Copernican revolution has not yet produced all of its effects on the masculine imagination.

—Luce Irigaray, "Toute Théorie du Sujet. . . ,"
Speculum De L'Autre Femme, Les Editions de Minuit, 1974, 165

I f we were to posit along with Luce Irigaray that all theories of the subject will always be appropriated in the masculine, then the feminist project of redefining the subject as overdetermined—by gender, class, race, ethnicity, nationality and other interacting social markers and relations—would appear conceptually futile and politically hopeless. Yet Irigaray's texts themselves, along with many other contemporary postmodernist and feminist works that critique the masculine-neutral universal subject, signal more nuanced, historicized and positive modes of critiquing and redefining subjectivity. In fact, it seems that announcing the death of the supposedly neutral universal subject does not leave a theoretical vacuum. Quite the contrary, it actually proliferates politicized formulations of subjectivity. This is not to say that the new definitions resemble the old ones. Rather than hiding their ideological biases under claims of universality, non-universalist or partial versions of the subject interweave philosophical, historical and political discourses in order to undermine and remap in a more egalitarian fashion the hierarchical social structures and relations that have buttressed the privileges of the universal subject and its representatives.

As we know, Western definitions of the universal subject have been historically inseparable from political definitions of citizenship. In a circular but mediated fashion, citizenship has been predicated upon the exercise of a supposedly universal "reason," while reasoning was predicated upon the exercise of civic and political functions. During the past thirty years, scholars have illustrated how definitions of reason and, by extension, access to the rights and privileges of democratic citizenship are inseparable from the complex power hierarchies and relations that formerly excluded large groups of people from citizenship and still exclude them today from proportional political power and representation. Hence, current postmodernist and feminist critiques of universal subjectivity are inseparable from the ideological objectives of undermining the prerogatives of historically privileged subjects and the institutional structures and symbolic strategies that sustain or disseminate their power. Such a complex task requires not so much eliminating the subject in a voluntaristic fashion by declaring its death, but exercising a very delicate balance between de-constructing and re-constructing subjectivity. As Foucault himself has illustrated, claiming that the universal subject is dead is only the rhetorical beginning of the difficult philosophical and political process of modifying exclusionary or dominative political and symbolic structures and relations. The rest—including examining what kind of subject is allegedly dead, who or what plots its death and why, and what kind of subjectivity survives or can be generated in its stead—is the rigorous work that, following the leads of postmodernist theorists and activists, needs to be pursued.

In principle, the concept of the universal subject, delineated and implemented by Greek philosophy and politics and reformulated by Enlightenment rationalism and (post-) revolutionary politics, reserves differences among subjects to the private sphere. The private sphere constitutes a female-centered but male-regulated domain where affect and particularities can be expressed in specific fashions, depending upon one's national, ethnic, or racial "identities" as well as upon one's age and gender. By contrast, formulations of universal subjectivity begin with the premise that the public sphere offers a forum where neutral, absolute and identical subject-citizens identify their common good. Ideally—since universality is a regulative ideal to be approximated, not a reality that can be fully attained—all individual or group interests, tastes, identifications or affiliations must be bracketed from the public sphere and relegated to the private sphere.

Nevertheless, the supposedly universal citizen-subjects interacting in the public sphere are themselves a product of determinate political processes of both internal and external selection. In practice, and often in theory as well, they comprise a highly privileged and preselected group of "rational" and, most often, empowered men. According to most universalist paradigms, these masculine-neutral subjects are the only beings deemed capable and worthy of expressing and representing the general interests of the *polis* or, later, of the modern nation-state. Women, slaves, ethnic and racial minorities, and the working classes all tend to be more or less historically and conceptually excluded from full citizenship and, correlatively, from privileged definitions of subjectivity. These prerequisite exclusions from subjectivity and from full political rights and representation constitute the enabling paradox of the so-called all-inclusive, abstract and generally representative universal subject. It seems that the ancient and the modern universalist citizen-subjects, despite their significant historical differences, share one important feature. Both can be universal only insofar as they are irredeemably particular: that is, insofar as they symbolically and politically represent the interests and ideals of a highly privileged and determinate community of (usually) men deemed capable of exercising the most consecrated and powerful socio-political and cultural functions.

Postmodernist and feminist scholarship point out the constitutive exclusions and contradictions of so-called universal subjectivity. Reacting against universalist paradigms, postmodernist scholarship privileges the particular qualities and partial political affiliations that universalist philosophy claims to, without being able to, extricate from the public sphere. Thus, in order to undermine the prerogatives of universalist conceptions of subjectivity, postmodernist scholarship emphasizes the heterogeneity and mutability of subjects, the specific political interests that motivate their actions, and the irreconcilable differences that divide overdetermined gendered, ethnic, racial, sexual or national communities in democratic societies. According to postmodernist theorists like Jean-François Lyotard, these political differences among groups and individuals preclude arbitration and consensus, two of the most important ways of establishing the validity of claims according to rationalist universalist paradigms.

These valuable postmodern critiques undoubtedly enrich our understanding of the limits and inherent contradictions of universal subjectivity. Nevertheless, insofar as they propose to offset the absolutism of universality with the equivalent absolutism of radical particularity, they risk undermining their original goals. As Robert Fraisse argues, "As for differentialism, it is a reaction to universalism and to its individualist version. It is supposed to break with the assimilatory and hegemonic propensity of the subject. But in order to do so, it has no choice but to absolutize differences, to the point that different subjects manifest themselves as so many absolute subjects."[1] The absolutization of differences can easily turn into its logical contrary, the relativization of differences. Paradoxically, an indiscriminate focus upon heterogeneity and differences within and among subjects tends to relativize differences in two main ways. It either explicitly presents all differences as equivalent in importance, validity, and nature, or it does so implicitly by producing no criteria or institutionalized processes for distinguishing among them. This cultural relativism defeats the postmodernist objective of being sensitive to differences and, insofar as it is possible, of providing the socio-political conditions in which they can be expressed and negotiated.

Even more dangerously, the relativization of differences can inadvertently support identitarian or (neo)communitarian ethics, the very historically essentialist forma-tions that postmodern critiques generally seek to displace. If no rational means of distinguishing among validity claims are offered, or if, furthermore, all differences are indiscriminately celebrated, what is to prevent, for example, neo-communitarian eth-nic or religious groups from violently imposing internal group homogeneity or from waging war with other groups in the name of irreconcilable cultural differences? As the sociological and political research of the group of scholars who contributed to the recent work *Penser le Sujet* illustrates so well, a sobering look at the rhetoric and prac-tices of fundamentalist groups should suffice to indicate the dangers of radically differentialist paradigms.[2] This research also serves to reveal absolutist differentialist paradigms as sometimes complicit with the logic of universalism, which, albeit for opposite reasons, forcibly assumes or imposes internal group-based homogeneity.

With these critiques in mind, I would argue that a model of subjectivity which cor-responds more closely to the postmodernist political objectives of encouraging respect for (inter)subjective differences depends in part upon safeguarding those elements of rationalist universalist ethics that enable us to differentiate among differences. The main goal of this collection of essays is to contribute to the delineation of such a medi-ating path by critically examining and borrowing from both modernist and post-modernist versions of subjectivity that structure the landscape of much contemporary scholarship and political rhetoric. Thus, in the course of five interrelated yet relatively independent essays, this work examines some of the ways in which Enlightenment and postmodernist theories constantly negotiate the boundaries and tensions between universalist and particularist socio-political paradigms in their definitions of the sub-ject and, relatedly, in their construction of public and private spheres.

The book follows a concentric structure. It begins with an essay which focuses upon modernist and postmodernist depictions of the microstructure of the single subject by comparing and juxtaposing the universalist model of subjectivity pro-vided by Rousseau with the more fluid and heterogeneous models provided, during very different historical moments, by Diderot and by several important postmod-ernist scholars. The second essay considers the larger structure of gendered intersubjectivity from the perspective of Luce Irigaray's model of dialogic interac-tion among "sexuate" subjects.

The next two essays analyze depictions of the macrostructure of the networks of power relations that govern collective behavior. The first of these employs the works of Nancy Fraser and Judith Butler in order to critically consider Habermas's ratio-nalist paradigm of communicative action and its applicability in (the) democratic public sphere(s). The fourth essay attempts to expand the horizons of definitions of the subject even further by relying upon Pierre Bourdieu's and Griselda Pollock's critique of Kantian universalist aesthetics in order to identify some of the connections and mediations between the fields of "high" culture and politics.

In the conclusion, I consider some of the structural and conceptual features of Enlightenment and contemporary democratic theories that contribute to gender-based disadvantage in their definitions of subject-citizenship, and propose a formulation of group-based subject-citizenship, that is more egalitarian in nature. Since micro- and macro-structures of subjectivity are inextricably interrelated, the concentric organization of this book, which begins with a consideration of the single subject and leads up to an analysis of the networks of power relations among subjects, is mostly formal. Nevertheless, this organization provides a useful way of "logically" building up to the main objective of this project, that of analyzing politically useful models of collective interaction among subjects in democratic societies.

Throughout these essays I propose a "mediating" model which accepts the heterogeneity and social overdetermination of single subjects and the differences among (groups of) subjects argued for by postmodernist scholars, without abandoning the procedures necessary for collective deliberations within public spheres provided by some rationalist universalist paradigms. Moreover, remaining above all sensitive to feminist critiques of the masculinist universal subject, I argue that models of (inter)subjectivity must not simply delineate abstract and isolated subjects, but must also open forums of communication among diverse, concrete, and as it now stands, hierarchically positioned communities.

Such a project entails a philosophical, political, historical, and symbolic venture. It involves not only acknowledging (for example) Woman as a co-subject in dialogue, but providing the conditions of possibility for women to identify themselves—and to be acknowledged by men—as subjects of history on a par with men. This does not mean that women have to claim the same sort of subjectivity—unitary, conscious, transcendental, universal, and/or essentialized —that (some) men have, at least philosophically speaking, recently rejected. Quite the contrary, it means viewing and analyzing both women and men as participants in the social, symbolic, and political order without strictly defining or hypostasizing their multidetermined individual and collective social identities. In other words, it means openly redefining the subject in a manner that does not reduce either men or women to the status of objects, but enables both to function as sexual subjects who share political, social and cultural power in the context of truly, and not only formally or nominally, democratic societies.

NOTES

1   Robert Fraisse's essay, *"Pour une politique des sujets singuliers,"* can be found in the anthology *Penser le Sujet: Autour d'Alain Touraine*, Colloque de Cérisy, directed by François Dubet and Michel Wieviorka. Paris: Fayard, 1995, 560.

2   *Ibid.* I am specifically alluding to Nilüfer Göle's analysis of Islamist movements in Turkey and North Africa in his essay *"L'Emergence du sujet islamique,"* to Cathrine Delacroix's

analysis of the disastrous socio-political effects of the resurgence of Islamist movements upon Algerian and Egyptian women in her essay "*Algériennes et Egyptiennes: Enjeux et sujets de société en crise,*" and to Gilles Kepel's exposition of the essentialist and dangerous cultural logic of neo-communitarian politics in his study of the Rushdie affair in his essay, "*Entre société et communauté: Les musulmans au Royaume-Uni et en France aujourd'hui.*"

THE TROPE OF DISSIMULATION

one

CONSTRUCTING AND DECONSTRUCTING
SEXUAL AND POLITICAL ECONOMIES
DURING THE FRENCH ENLIGHTENMENT

I n *The Postmodern Condition*,[1] Jean-François Lyotard associates the "Enlightenment narrative" with the postulate of "a possible unanimity between rational minds [. . .] in which the hero of knowledge works toward a good ethico-political end-universal peace"(6). In contradistinction to this type of totalizing "metanarrative," Lyotard provisionally defines postmodernism as "[an] incredulity toward metanarratives" that "refines our sensitivity to differences and reinforces our ability to tolerate the incommensurable. Its principle is not the expert's homology, but the inventor's paralogy"(6). The principle of homology identifies or produces a structured similarity. By contrast, the principle of paralogy disperses any kind of unitary or unifying signification into multiple truth-effects. The production of such effects takes place within a system of language that, contrary to conventional belief, does not provide the means of communicating "truths" about a commonly agreed-upon transcendental or empirical reality. Instead, it provides a field of performative speech-acts which "fall into the domain of a general agonistics."(10) In other words, according to Lyotard, truth is an effect of competing and conventionally agreed upon rhetorical strategies—some of which are more effective than others—rather than an objective reality which (some) human beings can identify.

On the one hand, if we were to accept Lyotard's narrative about the Enlightenment, which perceives the discourses of this period primarily through the optic of Kantian philosophy, it would then appear that the rules of the game have practically reversed from the eighteenth century to the present. On the other hand, we could also read the heterogeneous narratives of the French (rather than the German) Enlightenment as dramatizing performative rather than cohesive identities and deploying strategies of dissimulation rather than offering mimetic representations of an underlying "reality." In this case, Lyotard's opposition between the Enlightenment and postmodernism would cease to be persuasive as a depiction of Enlightenment thought while continuing to function as a highly effective platform of contrast or subversion for his postmodernist theories. Yet both approaches—those which mark a complete rupture between modernism and postmodernism, and those which establish only fluid continuities between them—may hide some aspects of the "truth."

As a point of entrance into this debate, I would like to suggest that an analysis of the ways in which the trope of *dissimulation* simultaneously functioned both to establish and radically subvert a sexual division of spheres during the late eighteenth century can help us identify some of the historical ruptures and continuities between the discourses of the French Enlightenment and postmodern/poststructuralist theories. This essay argues that the trope of dissimulation, which we will symptomatically analyze in Diderot's and Rousseau's works, contributes significantly both to the formulation and subversion of a new kind of republican civic and political order. In this new order, the main axis of social distinction—and, potentially, of social transgression—is no longer the vertical hierarchy between the aristocracy and the people. Instead, republican society is primarily organized around the supposedly horizontal—but nevertheless asymmetrical—complementarity between women and men, or more generally, between private and public spheres. Thus, on one hand, this essay supports Lyotard's argument that the discourses of the French Enlightenment establish the foundations for the socio-political and gendered organization of contemporary western societies rather than engaging in postmodern subversions, fragmentations or displacements of subjectivity. On the other hand, this essay also identifies in some of Rousseau's and many of Diderot's principal works some striking continuities with the postmodern project of displacing stable sexual, and more generally socio-political, economies.

The concept of "dissimulation," as its etymology suggests, is based upon the double valence of the word *simulare*, which signifies to copy or reproduce an object in a seemingly faithful fashion that actually feigns, covers-up or distorts the "original" object being represented. Already this formulation invokes the much critiqued notion of an "original" object whose "reality" or "truth value" is artfully distorted by inferior and deceptive reproductions. However, while hierarchies which uphold such "metaphysics of presence" may continue to function in the Enlightenment texts we will examine, they are undermined by the competing (or agonistic) existence of alternative assumptions which are currently associated with the movement of postmodernism. For example, we will encounter in some Enlightenment texts the postulate that acts of imitation do not necessarily depend upon the presence of "originals." They can be imitations of imitations (*simulacra*) whose origins are exposed as mythological or ideological constructions. We will also encounter the analogous postulate that "dissimulation" does not necessarily entail the distortion of an otherwise self-evident and objective truth. Instead, it can function as a disruptive and sometimes gender-coded (in the feminine) rhetorical strategy that produces only the illusion of a stable, objective, and humanly ascertainable reality.

It goes without saying that the purpose of this comparison between Enlightenment and postmodernist narratives is not to obscure the significant historical and methodological differences between them. Nor does this essay intend to deny the even greater economic and technological differences that distinguish early and late capitalist societies. Rather, the goal of this comparison is to employ postmodernist assumptions to illuminate selected French Enlightenment works and, conversely, to employ Enlightenment works to highlight some of the assumptions and strategies of specific postmodernist and poststructuralist theories. Moreover, by retrieving some of the agonistic discursive relations of French Enlightenment thought and practices, we can see that the stability and lasting influence of a republican politics based upon a universalist-rationalist cultural logic and a sharply gendered division of spheres was not as evident then as it may currently seem, with historical hindsight, to contemporary postmodernist scholars.

1. THE REPUBLICAN ORDER

As feminist scholars have demonstrated during the past thirty years, a sexual division of spheres between a masculinized public sphere and a feminized private sphere is constitutive of the eighteenth-century republican order.[2] The role of women in republican discourses was ambiguous—or more precisely—ambivalent. Women came to be perceived both as a potential problem and as a potential solution to the problems of the still fragile developing democracy. On the one hand, as Rousseau's discourses illustrate particularly well, women's regulation of the domestic sphere could serve as an indispensable supplement to men's political regulation of the bourgeois public sphere. In their roles as wives, mothers, and educators, bourgeois women fulfilled their civic duties by reproducing and reinforcing the values and norms of the newly instituted republican order. However, once women's civic participation became directly political rather than mediated through their nurturing or support of children and men, women were depicted as dangerous sources of sexual, and hence also socio-political, disorder.

As Dominique Godineau has documented, the exclusion of women from the republican public sphere was, paradoxically enough, partially justified in terms of women's direct political role in the French Revolution. Acting as initiators of popular rebellion, "in 1795, as in 1789 and May 1793, women occupied the streets in the weeks before the insurrection. They assembled in force (on May 23, 1795, the deputies prohibited them from gathering in groups of more than five on pain of arrest) and called men to action, branding those who refused 'cowards.'"[3] Shortly after the Revolution, the masculine order was more firmly consolidated than it had been during the *Ancien Régime*. Women were denied civil and political rights, including the right to group together in all-female private clubs or in the streets; the right to participate in deliberative assemblies or in local committees and political groups; and even the privilege of running prestigious salons, on the grounds that such a semi-public display of knowledge would hideously masculinize them. In brief, women were denied the explicit rights and unarticulated privileges that went along with the new democratic citizenship granted to men.

The denial of these rights was rationalized by means of a series of discourses that depicted women as less rational and more "natural" beings than "civilized" western men. These discourses attempted to present women as potential problems for the nascent and still precarious democratic order. Such misogynist descriptions took various and sometimes contradictory forms. In some republican discourses, women were depicted as disorderly, politically conservative, dogmatically religious, and supportive of the monarchy. As Lynn Hunt illustrates in her study of the propaganda organized around the figure of Marie Antoinette—who became a symbol of all women who defied republican gender norms—women were considered to be easily manipulable and manipulative, sexually corrupt, and deceptive. However, at the same time that they were accused of political conservatism, women were also accused of political radicalism. When their participation in the Revolution was acknowledged, it was depicted as inflammatory, disorganized, decadent, and irrational. In other words, it was depicted as unfit for a new democratic society seeking a stable and orderly political organization. According to Lynn Hunt, women's assimilation to aristocratic mores, often achieved by means of the trope of dissimulation, played a central role in all of these ideological depictions:

> Dissimulation was [. . .] an especially important theme in the denunciations of the queen. The ability to conceal one's true emotions, to act one way in public and another in private, was repeatedly denounced as the chief characteristic of court life and aristocratic manner in general. These relied above all on appearances, that is, the disciplined and self-conscious use of the body as a mask. The republicans, consequently, valued transparency—the unmediated expression of the heart—above all other personal qualities. Transparency was the perfect fit between public and

The Trope of Dissimulation

private; transparency was a body that told no lies and kept no secrets. It was the definition of virtue, and as such it was imagined to be critical to the future of the republic. Dissimulation, in contrast, threatened to undermine the republic: it was the chief ingredient in every conspiracy; it lay at the heart of the counterrevolution. [. . .] Dissimulation was also described in the eighteenth century as a characteristic feminine quality, not just an aristocratic one. According to Montesquieu and Rousseau, it was women who taught men how to dissimulate, how to hide their true feelings in order to get what they wanted in the public arena. The salon was the most important site of this teaching [and educated women their target], and it was also the one place where society women could enter the public sphere. In a sense, then, women in public were (like prostitutes) synonymous with dissimulation, with the gap between public and private.[4]

While the direct social and political participation of women in the public sphere was portrayed as a problem for a developing fraternal republican society, by contrast, the domestic functions of women in the private sphere were presented as a stabilizing force for the republican order. Evidently, both kinds of discourses—those which praised domestic women and those which criticized public women—represented the female sex as closer to nature than the male sex. However, public women supposedly reflected the more dangerous, unruly aspects of nature which threatened the masculinized civil and political order. By contrast, domestic women supposedly reflected the nurturing, maternal aspects of "mother" Nature which served both as a foundation and as a complement to a masculinized culture. Rousseau's influential republican discourses hinge upon these two diverging connotations of feminized Nature. As we will see, despite their apparent contradiction, these descriptions of naturalized femininity—and of feminized Nature—buttress from two different sides the same hierarchical gendered division of spheres.

For example, wishing to reform "civilization" in a manner that approaches it to what he considers the positive aspects of "Nature," Rousseau argues, "[The arts and sciences] stifle in men's breasts that sense of original liberty, for which they seem to have been born; cause them to love their own slavery, and so make of them what is called a civilized people."[5] In this work, it seems that (mother) Nature is defined as an initial state from which culture was (immaculately?) conceived. This state of Nature is characterized by valorized cultural attributes such as "liberty," "sympathy," and uncorrupted "maternal origins." Conversely, "civilization" is characterized by negative attributes such as "slavery," "effeminacy" (which conflates aristocratic and public feminine codes), and "selfishness." However, when attempting to propose an explanatory mythology of the transition from nature to culture, Rousseau runs into problems and self-contradictions. For if (mother) Nature was initially so peaceful and perfect, then how and why did culture develop? And if the effeminate aristocratic culture is so irretrievably corrupt, then why does Rousseau insist upon salvaging numerous aspects of it instead of proposing a full-fledged return to (mother) Nature? In addition, given the fact that the author's depictions of Nature are expressed solely in terms of cultural attributes, does Rousseau consider a return to "Nature" possible or even imaginable?

To confuse this binary opposition between (the right kind of) maternal Nature and (the wrong kind of) effeminate aristocratic Culture even further, it is worth pointing out that Rousseau not only reverses the hierarchical terms of his Nature/Culture dichotomy in two of his major political texts, *A Discourse on the Origin of Inequality* and *The Social Contract*, but also masculinizes the formerly feminized sexual codes of this opposition:

> Savage, indolent, and perpetually accompanied by danger, the savage cannot be fond of sleep; his sleep too must be light, like that of the animals, which think but little and may be said to slumber all the time they do not think. Self-preservation being his chief and almost sole concern, he must exercise most those faculties which are most concerned with attack or defense, either for overcoming his prey, or for preventing him from becoming prey of other animals. (*A Discourse on the Origin of Inequality*, 58)

> I suppose men to have reached the point at which the obstacles in the way of their preservation in the state of nature show their power of resistance to be greater than the resources at the disposal of each individual for his maintenance in that state. That primitive condition can then subsist no longer; and the human race would perish unless it changed its manner of existence. (*The Social Contract*, 190)

As these two citations reveal, in setting the stage for his social contract, Rousseau seems to privilege the regulative powers of a masculinized republican culture over a momentarily Hobbesian depiction of (also virile or at least masculine-neutral) Nature. Nevertheless, the distinction between Nature and Culture is not as clear as it may initially appear. According to Nancy Armstrong's Althusserian reading of Rousseau's social contract, the moment of transition from nature to culture is always already cultural. Contractarian ethics assume a rational and collective political process among "primitive" men who are already sufficiently civilized and individuated to form a mutually beneficial and orderly society. Hence, in contractarian narratives, the myth of a masculine republican Culture emerging from the best elements of a feminized mother Nature imperceptibly changes into the myth of mother Nature already assuming, *in potentia*, a virile republican cultural form. In Nancy Armstrong's words,

> the power of the contract depended not so much on the logic of exchange as on the figurative power of the contract to constitute the very parties it proposed to regulate. [. . .] Something must be there from the beginning to individuate and direct each man's desire toward the common good.[. . .] It can be argued that the contract provides the central trope of Enlightenment discourse, which always creates what it seems to organize and individuates what it seems to unify.[6]

The Trope of Dissimulation

On the one hand, Rousseau depicts an idealized republican and virile civilization which is nevertheless imperfect enough to require maternal "naturalization." On the other hand, he posits a "savage" and agonistic virile state of nature which is nevertheless ideal enough to be composed of already rational and individuated republican men. While, along with Derrida, we could view these two versions of the Nature/Culture dichotomy as entailing ideological aporias—since their binary formulations are mutually exclusive yet equally plausible (and hence, undecidable)—they nevertheless provide a coherent worldview. Taken together, these binary oppositions between Nature and Culture represent a semi-democratic and masculine political order which takes away from women some of the "complementary" powers it originally appears to invest them with.

In his analysis of Rousseau's supplementary paradigms, Derrida claims to reveal the blind spots of Rousseau's writing: "The concept of the supplement is a sort of blind spot in Rousseau's text, the not-seen that opens and limits visibility."[7] Yet in his reading Derrida himself could be perceived as implanting, rather than merely identifying, the supposed blind spots into Rousseau's text. This hypothesis becomes persuasive if we take into consideration the fact that Rousseau himself declares his (or any) notion of a "state of nature" to be an indispensible mythological construct of an irretrievable moment which may never have existed:

> What experiments would have to be made, to discover the natural man? And how are those experiments to be made in a state of society? So far am I from undertaking to solve this problem, that I think I have sufficiently considered the subject, to venture to declare beforehand that our greatest philosophers would not be too good to direct such experiments, and our most powerful sovereigns to make them. (*A Discourse on the Origin of Inequality*, 45)

Derrida and other deconstructive critics argue that Rousseau's texts contain competing interpretations that displace univocal meanings into contradictory and undecidable traces. Moreover, these critics seem to assume that the author—or, to avoid the so-called intentional fallacy, his text—is "blind" to his/its narrative slippages and contradictions. Such assumptions make possible and appealing the intervention of deconstructive methods of reading. While it would be pointless to claim that Rousseau himself practiced "deconstruction," it seems that both he and Derrida displace the hierarchical binary oppositions they initially establish in order to construct various ideological fictions. However, while Derrida's methods work to displace stable signification, Rousseau's seemingly irreconcilable ideological fictions work toward a common and identifiable set of goals. As we have seen, Rousseau's narratives sometimes implicitly and at other times explicitly attempt to destabilize an aristocratic culture, which they devalorize as decadent and feminine, by instituting a virile republican culture where domestic(ated) versions of femininity supplement a new democratic brotherhood among men.

2. THE REPUBLICAN DISORDER

Although Rousseau and Diderot may have disagreed on certain important issues, Diderot did not view his version of republican discourse as opposite of or mutually exclusive to Rousseau's. Nevertheless, Diderot's scientific innovations in empirical modes of social and physical analysis, combined with his more open interpretations of sexual and political economies, render him less the forefather of modern rational(ist) and virile democratic societies than the inspiration for the postmodernist displacement of stable sexual and political economies. In this section, we will examine the ways in which Diderot's displacement of rationalist scientific paradigms had profound implications upon his alternative, non-rationalist—though certainly not irrational—and fluid formulations of gendered subjectivity.

As is often pointed out, eighteenth-century *philosophes*, who typically engaged in a number of (for them) interrelated intellectual pursuits ranging from science and philosophy to literature and politics, were profoundly influenced by the scientific quest for truth-certainty undertaken by René Descartes. In his simultaneously theosophical and scientific writings, Descartes traced what he considered to be the vast difference between truth and error. On the one hand, truth provided "clear" and "distinct" ideas whose accuracy was guaranteed by God. On the other hand, error was manifested through sensations which resembled true perceptions—such as hallucinations, dreams, or day dreams—but were actually illusions generated by the unreliable sense-perceptions and passions. Already we see sketched in this formulation a hierarchical opposition between mind and body. While conscious reason can provide access to undistorted truth, somatic and emotive experiences result, for the most part, in error.

For contemporary critics as well as for Descartes's contemporaries, this hierarchical binary opposition proved somewhat problematic. For example, in her intelligent and sensitive letters to Descartes, Princess Elizabeth of Bohemia raises a crucial question. If the mind is strictly immaterial and the body material, then how can the mind govern the body or, conversely, the body influence the mind? In brief, how can the two types of (material and immaterial) entities interact? It seems that the method of logical deduction has left some epistemological gaps which only the scientific method of induction, through its reliance upon "external" or perceptible signs of the body as manifestations of "states of mind," might be able to resolve. According to Elizabeth and other critics, Descartes unsuccessfully attempted to follow deductive and, less so, inductive reasoning in order to interpret the signs of passions as symptoms of the mind in *Les Passions de l'Âme*. However, some of the empiricist philosophes, and particularly Denis Diderot, took this challenge further than Descartes or other rationalist thinkers imagined was possible or desirable.

Throughout his scientific discourses on perception, including *Lettres sur les aveugles* and *Lettre sur les sourds et les muets*, Diderot sought to examine and sharpen human sensory

The Trope of Dissimulation

experience. Unlike Descartes, who remained loyal to his hierarchy of mind over body and continued to begin his investigations with the phenomenological experiences of the mind, Diderot began his investigations with the body—and often ended with it as well—in order to better understand the mind. In fact, it is not even clear that Diderot maintained, though he certainly conceptually relied upon, the rationalist mind-body distinction. For example, in his observations of the behavior of a gifted young woman who was blind, Diderot noted with respect and wonder how her "mental" faculties—like her mathematical ability, her artistic sensitivity, and her memory—sharpened as a result of being deprived of the conventional modes of perception which have conditioned and restricted the behavior of women. Following her premature death, Diderot ruefully remarked, "With such a prodigious memory and a penetration the equal of her memory, what heights would she have not reached in the sciences, had she been accorded a longer life!"[8] Here Diderot implies that biological human faculties are similar in both sexes and that sexual difference, which turns out to disadvantage women, is socially produced. By means of this "empirical" method of testing the development of different modes of "seeing," Diderot imperceptibly makes the transition from discourses of nature (like physiology and neurology) to discourses of culture (like history and sociology) in a manner that presents nature as fully inscribed by gender-based cultural norms. In so doing, he also implicitly criticizes the gendered division of spheres that represented women as closer to nature and men as closer to culture.

Diderot examined the complex processes involved in enacting and changing social roles—as opposed to accepting commonplace assumptions regarding universal or naturalized social structures and identities—not only in his scientific and epistemological discourses, but also in his fiction. For instance, nowhere are social identities and relations figured as more consistently paradoxical and unstable than in Le Neveu de Rameau.[9] This narrative itself eludes all stable generic categorizations. Is it a novel? A drama? A philosophical dialogue? We can only claim that it a pastiche that combines all of the above—and perhaps also other—genres.[10] Significantly, Le Neveu de Rameau begins as a dialogue. A dialogue not simply in the sense of a conversation between two or more speakers, but in a Bakhtinian sense, which sets into play a multiplicity of diverse and often conflicting subject positions that simultaneously produce and undermine the effect of what could be called a coherent "human subjectivity."

The narrator claims, "I converse with myself about politics, love, taste or philosophy. I abandon my mind to all its licentiousness." (43) Comparing his aleatory ideas to "laughing and lively-eyed courtesans"(43) chased by his philandering mind, the narrator initially tempts us with the conventional mind-body dichotomy only to subsequently deconstruct it. First he reverses its terms by privileging bodily desire over the mind. Then he displaces the dichotomy altogether by speaking of the mind in terms of bodily pleasures and of bodily pleasures in terms of the mind. Thus, even though in order to lend credibility to his characterization of Rameau's nephew as "one of the most bizarre personages in a land where God has provided no lack of them," (46) the implied narrator continually attempts to present himself as a comparatively average *bonhomme*, he cannot be said to embody the stable frame of reference he strives to represent. Following the narrator's initial internal monologue, the readers cannot discern if—or to what extent—the paradoxical figure of Rameau's nephew is a product of the narrator's dialogic imagination or a textual "referent." In this context, the whole notion of stable cultural and textual standards that would help readers assess the nephew's "bizarre" deviations becomes moot. Conventional norms and identities are provided only to be interrogated and subverted by Diderot's text and its readers.

For example, when depicting Rameau's nephew, the narrator continually invokes signifiers like "nature," "honesty," "good" and "bad," as if both he and the implied readers knew or could agree upon what these terms signified: "The notions of honesty and dishonesty must be quite oddly mixed up in his head, for he shows, without ostentation, that nature has bestowed him with good qualities, and, without shame, that he has also been given bad ones. Further, he is endowed with a strong sense of organization, a singular warmth of imagination, and uncommon lung power." (46) In every way the nephew is characterized as an exception to a norm which is always assumed and never elaborated. This norm is not even outlined in a local or subjective fashion, with reference to the nephew's underlying or foundational "identity" according to which his "deviating" behavior could be assessed. There can be no question of the existence of such a foundation presenting itself even as a myth—much less as a "reality"—once we find out that,

> Nothing is less like him than he himself is. Sometimes he is thin and gaunt, like someone suffering the last stages of consumption; you could count his teeth through his cheeks. You would think he hadn't eaten for days. . . . The next month, he is fat and plump, as if he had never left the financier's table. . . . Today, with dirty linen, covered in rags, almost with no shoes, . . . one is almost tempted to call him over and give him some alms. Tomorrow, powdered, shod, curled and well dressed, he walks with his head high, showing himself off. You would even take him for someone genteel. (46)

Since there is no grounding identity (a stable "he") from which we can ascertain how the nephew dissimulates "himself," in this case the notion of dissimulation itself cannot be viewed as entailing "an original" presence obscured by false imitations or "disingenuous" roles. In fact, the nephew's "identity" consists of nothing but the continuous production of heterogeneous and paradoxical roles. Nonetheless, it could be argued that paradox—or that which is beside (*para*) general opinion (*doxa*)—relies upon the implicit assumption that common opinions exist and could be generally identified.

In a limited and elusive fashion this text appears to present this sense of commonly shared opinions through the figure of the rather "unreliable" narrator. Through him, we intercept the uncannily panoptical glance of the audience of

The Trope of Dissimulation

readers who strategically appear and disappear under various generic subject-positions—*on* or *vous*—and seem to continually follow, survey, and judge Rameau's nephew. The rhetorical interchangeability between the hypothetical positions *on* and *vous* deliberately conflates the contemporaneous fictional public (*on*) who might judge the nephew according to "their" norms and the larger, transtemporal audience of implied readers (*vous*) who evaluate him according to an even more diverse and dynamic set of cultural standards. This conflation of (or undecidability between) two different sets of readers creates the (illusory) effect of universal standards of behavior which both a historically limited audience (*on*) and a vaster (ahistorical?) public (*vous*) could agree upon.

The fact that the narrator desires to produce the effect of stable norms becomes even more evident in his attempts to include himself in those generic positions while differentiating himself from Rameau's nephew through repeated qualifications like, "I have no esteem for those kinds of 'originals.'" (47) Nevertheless, even for this self-declared "ordinary" representative of a general public, the lure of extra-ordinariness retains a seductive appeal: "They [these 'originals'] give me pause about once a year, when I encounter them, because their character is a departure from that of others, and they break with that fastidious uniformity which our education, social conventions, and proprieties of usage have brought about." (47) Once again we note that the narrator, who associated himself only a moment ago with certain stable norms, presently disavows those norms and returns to the dialogic instability we have observed at the beginning of his narration.

How can these vacillations—in the depictions of both characters—be deciphered? I would suggest that cannot do so by appealing to a coherent and rationalist structure of "value" and meaning. The clues to the alternative cultural logic elaborated by this text can be found in the thematized systems of signification which appear extra-linguistic: in the nephew's pantomimic gestures that versatilely mimic numerous, themselves imitative, socialized postures; in his vast dramatic repertoire of seemingly incompatible or paradoxical roles which defy the consolidation of conventional identities; and in his impassioned musical improvisations which elude univocal interpretations. In a social field which always already codes (and is coded by) our linguistic systems, be they in the form of words, movements, or bodily styles, there can be no question of "authentic" feelings or of "natural" behavior. Even the nephew's seemingly "natural" heterosexual predilection for women—whom he fetishizes according to prevalent norms into metonymic and metaphoric assemblages of "teeth, a row of pearls; eyes, feet, some skin, cheeks, teats, a hart's legs, shapely thighs and buttocks" (131)—enact and satirize the cumulative performances of gender identities that operate in a heterosexual matrix. As Judith Butler illustrates in *Gender Trouble*, this kind of parodic performance of gender roles helps interrogate and subvert the frequently naturalized categories of sex, gender, and (hetero)sexual orientation:

> If the ground of gendered identity is the stylized repetition of acts through time and not a seemingly seamless identity, then the spacial metaphor of a ground will be displaced and revealed as a stylized configuration. . . . That gender reality is created through sustained social performances means that the very notions of an essential sex and a true or abiding masculinity or femininity are also constituted as part of the strategy that conceals gender's performative character and the performative possibilities for proliferating gender configurations outside the restricting frames of masculinist domination and compulsory heterosexuality.[11]

If the nephew's repeated ironic impersonations of social roles or "identities" seem too subtle to expose their social construction and their mutable character, he makes these features more apparent by mimicking roles which would appear "unnatural" or incongruous for him but "natural" and appropriate for others. For example, when he describes his mistress to the narrator, "[he] began to mimic the way his wife walked, with little steps; he held his head up in the air; he fiddled with his fan; it was a charge of our little coquettes, most pleasant and most ridiculous." (131) Without much difficulty, the nephew dissimulates the gender roles conventionally deemed appropriate solely for women. Moreover, as we have already observed, he can reproduce with equal ease the "masculine" roles conventionally deemed appropriate only for men. In this parodic repetition, conventional norms of behavior lose the naturalized or universalized foundations which enabled their legitimation.

This kind of interrogation and displacement of the dichotomy between "real" sexual identities versus dissimulation and gender role-playing is accomplished in a somewhat different fashion in Diderot's *La Religieuse*.[12] By all appearances, this novel narrates the "truth" of sex and gender. Suzanne, the seemingly innocent heroine of the novel, falls victim to the social valorization of patrilineage by being ostracized by her family and forced into a convent as a result of being an "illegitimate" daughter. Subsequently, she also falls victim to the sexual and political corruption which infects the supposedly "pure" convent life. Hence, the readers are confronted with the "truth" of sex by two concentric narratives, both of which are related by Suzanne. By means of Suzanne's "secret" letters or memoirs to her "benefactor," M. le Marquis de Croismare, we catch a glimpse of the sexual politics of convent life. At the same time, these letters also enable readers to witness the panoptical surveillance of Suzanne's own body and behavior by various members of the convent. In other words, we have access both to Suzanne's sexuality and to the sexual behavior of the other convent sisters, from whom Suzanne attempts to differentiate herself. However, rather than revealing the "truth" of sex, both concentric and interdependent narratives strategically produce, or dissimulate, sexual truth-effects. In order to substantiate this claim, I will compare the rhetorical strategies at work in Suzanne's description of her imprisonment and surveillance in the convent with Foucault's carefully framed formulation of the Panopticon in *Discipline and Punish*.[13]

The Trope of Dissimulation

Never forgetting that she is writing to a male benefactor who is likely to be moved by her "femininity," Suzanne takes every opportunity to emphasize her feminine "charms." She repeatedly states that she is ostracized by her family because she is generally considered more beautiful than her "legitimate" sisters; she depicts in great detail the ways in which her convent sisters and mothers praise her appearance and desire her body; and she dwells upon her feminine frailness and the savage brutality with which her sisters physically abuse her once she refuses to conform to their "transgressive" sexual habits. In this sequence of narratives, the rhetoric of victimization—and its accompanying appeals to "frailness" or "dependency" upon men—conventionally serves the rhetoric of femininity and vice-versa. For example, in the scene where Suzanne's convent sisters flatter her physical appearance in order to manipulate her to join their monastery, both interrelated discourses—of feminization and of victimization—are at work:

My companions surrounded me. They took me in their arms, saying, "Sister, look how beautiful she is! Look how her veil brings out the fairness of her complexion! Look how becoming her headband is, how it rounds out her face and broadens her cheeks! Look how her habit shows off her waist and arms!" I was so desolate I could barely hear them. I must acknowledge, however, that when I was alone in my cell, I remembered their flattering remarks, and could not help checking them in my little mirror. It did seem to me that they were not completely out of place. (43)

In this scene, like in many others, the production of femininity and the exposure of the ploys that play and prey upon it depend upon the creation of expiatory truth-effects. These confessions employ rhetorical strategies similar to those detailed by Rousseau in his *Confessions*.[14] Much as Rousseau disculpates himself through his (in)famous account of his theft of the ribbon, Suzanne's confessions make her appear relatively innocent but vulnerable to corruption. In a similar but more modest fashion than Rousseau, who introduces his *Confessions* as "the only human portrait, painted exactly from nature and in all its truth, which exists or probably ever will exist," Suzanne prefaces her memoirs by stating, "I paint a part of my misfortunes, without talent or art, with the naiveté of a child of my age and the candor of my character." (39) Both narrators make emphatic claims to "truthful" and unmediated self-expression. These confessions supposedly represent their authors not only as unique or individual human beings, but also as representative of well-respected social types like "an honest man" and "an innocent woman."

As Paul de Man argues in *Allegories of Reading*, the very act of confession of minor flaws risks turning into a narrative intended to "exculpate the confessor, making the confession (and the confessional text) redundant as it originates." In both texts, self-justifications are framed in terms of tales of persecution, characterized by vast oscillations between paranoiac and narcissistic fantasies. Rousseau is surrounded everywhere by enemies—except during the moments in which he is worshiped by his friends and admirers. Similarly, Suzanne is trapped in a convent in which she is ostracized, hated, and labeled mad or "possessed by the devil" at all times when she is not the object of sexual desire by her convent sisters and mothers. Through her double narrative, Suzanne institutes rather than merely unveils what Foucault labels "the binary division and branding mad/sane, dangerous/harmless, normal/abnormal":

> Ever since that revolution had happened in my head, I was observed with more attention than ever. They followed me with their eyes; I could not make a move that was not watched; I could not say a word that was not weighed. They would come up to me to try and sound me out. They questioned me, and feigned commiseration and friendship. . . . Yet they would come into my cell at all hours, day or night, on some pretext or other, brusquely but silently. They would part the curtains, then draw away. (78)

Like Foucault in his formulation of the "Panopticon," Diderot sets up a political space where power functions by means of visual domination and the extraction of inner "secrets." These secrets generally concern the uses and abuses of the gendered body. However, the historicized narratives which reveal the mechanisms of power engage in tactical maneuvers similar to the power relations they claim to expose. Diderot stages the workings of power by enclosing his observant heroine in a monastery which institutes its disciplinary mechanisms in a panoptical fashion. For Foucault, the stage is provided by the hypothetical closure of a quarantined city under plague in which "[i]nspection functions ceaselessly" and "the gaze is alert everywhere" (*Discipline and Punish*, 195).

As David E. Bell points out, "The [disciplinary] techniques Foucault 'discovers' are, in fact, the very techniques he mobilizes as tools in his own research. The panoptical procedures he claims to unearth, moreover, figure metaphorically and quite strikingly theory's all-seeing gaze."[15] Through a series of well-chosen rhetorical moves, Foucault and Diderot do not merely depict but also enact their representations of power relations. In both cases, power is depicted from a space that bears the initial appearance of being external to the power relations it describes, but which actually constitutes—or at least simulates—the described networks and movements of power. Unlike Rousseau's narratives, Diderot's and Foucault's exposure and performance of the strategies that produce sexual economies do not sustain the hierarchies implicit in the republican sexual division of spheres. On the contrary, Foucault and Diderot mimic the institutional structures that produce or safeguard conventional gender roles in order to undermine naturalized gender asymmetries.

By analyzing the uses of the trope of dissimulation in influential French Enlightenment narratives, this essay has accentuated some of the ideological and rhetorical strategies these texts share with contemporary theoretical models like Lyotard's paralogy, Derrida's *supplément*, and Foucault's Panopticon. In so doing, it traced some of the ruptures and continuities between the two movements in their

The Trope of Dissimulation

definitions and subversions of sexual economies. As is the case with contemporary discourses, the Enlightenment texts that help organize sexual economies operate within a heterogeneous field of ideological relations which contradict, subvert, and sometimes reinforce one another. Retrospectively, we can plausibly argue that the kinds of republican discourses proposed by Rousseau, which continue to structure the sexual and political organization of contemporary democratic societies, have partly won out over the more fluid and fragmentary models of social and sexual identity proposed by Diderot. However, during the French Enlightenment the outcome of the agonistics between relatively closed and relatively open models of sexual and political identities, though perhaps not undecidable, was far from decided and, as we know all too well, these ideological struggles continue to this very day.

NOTES

1 *The Postmodern Condition: A Report on Knowledge.* Manchester: Manchester University Press, 1986.

2 This division of spheres is not symmetrical. The feminized private sphere served and complemented the social and political needs of the larger, masculinized public sphere.

3 "Daughters of Liberty and Revolutionary Citizens," trans. Arthur Goldhammer, 15–33, found in the anthology *A History of Women in the West,* vol. IV, edited by Michelle Perrot and Geneviève Fraisse. Cambridge: Harvard University Press, 1993, 16.

4 Lynn Hunt, *The Family Romance of the French Revolution.* Berkeley: University of California Press, 1992, 96–98.

5 *Discourse on the Arts and Sciences.* For all of the citations of Rousseau's political discourses, I am using the anthology *The Social Contract and Discourses,* trans. G. D. H. Cole. London: Everyman, 1973.

6 Nancy Armstrong, *Desire and Domestic Fiction.* London: Oxford University Press, 1986.

7 Jacques Derrida, *Of Grammatology,* trans. Gayatri Chakravorty Spivak. Baltimore: Johns Hopkins University Press, 1977, 163.

8 Denis Diderot, *Additions à la lettre sur les aveugles.* Paris: GF Flammarion, 1972, 137.

9 *Le Neveu de Rameau.* Paris: GF Flammarion, 1991.

10 Not accidentally, pastiche is presented as a preeminently postmodernist "style" by numerous contemporary critics, most notably by Frederic Jameson.

11 Judith Butler, *Gender Trouble.* New York: Routledge, 1988, 141.

12 Denis Diderot, *La Religieuse.* Paris: GF Flammarion, 1991.

13 *Discipline and Punish,* trans. Alan Sheridan. New York: Vintage Books, "Panopticism," 195–230.

14 J. J. Rousseau, *Confessions.* Paris: GF Flammarion,1987.

15 David Bell, *Circumstances: Chance in the Literary Text.* Lincoln: University of Nebraska Press, 1993, 53.

SEXUAL SUBJECTS

LUCE IRIGARAY'S ECONOMY OF
GENDERED INTERSUBJECTIVITY

I n *Speculum of the Other Woman*, Luce Irigaray casts a probing retrospective
glance at the phallocentric aspects of Western thought, beginning with
Freudian theory and ending with Platonic philosophy. In this and other works, she
critiques the negative consequences of defining sexual difference "by giving a priori
value to [masculine] Sameness." This kind of definition presents femininity only as
a distorted, lacking, or lesser mirror image of masculinity. Consequently, Irigaray
protests both prescriptive and descriptive definitions of the masculine and feminine
"subjects," which she finds are inextricably implicated in the masculine "production of a truth and of a meaning that are excessively univocal." (*This Sex Which is Not
One*, 78) Nevertheless, she undertakes the delicate and difficult task of "redefin[ing]

this language work that would leave space for the feminine" in a new economy of sexual difference. (*This Sex*, 78) This essay will explore Irigaray's ethics of sexual difference in order to assess how she reconstructs "the [gendered] subject" within a field of reciprocal intersubjective relations without falling prey to her own critiques of universalist or essentialist subjectivity.

From a conventional perspective, the question of what unites the category of "women" and distinguishes it from the category of "men" seems so obvious that it is considered a laughable or absurd question. The answer provided is almost always a positivist-empiricist one: just look and see! Yet neither the question nor this kind of answer seem so obvious from the point of view of feminist scholarship, which seeks precisely to contest and modify conventional and naturalized gender-based norms. On the one hand, from a constructionist point of view, this question remains unsatisfactorily answered by the axiomatic postulation of an ontological or naturalized notion of sexual difference. Such answers not only risk duplicating the gender hierarchy which depends upon essentialist definitions of sexual difference, but also beg the question altogether. They tend to "answer" the questions, "How is sexual difference inculcated and what are its effects" by means of different versions of the tautological formula, "Sexual difference is sexual difference." No matter how this formula is specifically filled out, the descriptions remain unsatisfying because of their underlying circular structure.

On the other hand, as we know equally well from differentialist and historicist critiques of radical constructionism, the feminist theories which deplore gender-based domination while at the same time completely disassociating the cultural metaphors of femininity and masculinity from the hierarchical power relations between actual men and women also run into theoretical and ideological impasses. What good is the subversive manipulation of these tropes if the levels of mediation—and contact—between them and concrete gender-based norms and practices are so distant as to be almost non-existent? According to my selective reading of her works, Irigaray mediates between the twin problematics of radical essentialism and radical constructionism. Her works outline an ambisexual ethics where gender is neither eliminated as a category used to identify, critique, and transform gender-based domination, nor posited as an essentialized and exclusive signifier of social difference.

According to Irigaray, in order to change the way we think about, understand, and live gender relations, we must first change the way we define and ask questions about sexual difference. Conventionally, sexual difference has been perceived as the distinction, whether natural or social, between the identities of men and women. These identities have not been defined in a symmetrical fashion. Usually, women have been defined in relation to the various socio-political objectives that were proposed and served the needs of (generally privileged) men. Irigaray desires to change this asymmetrical and androcentric framework. She argues that to even ask, "What is sexual difference?" is to broach this issue from a masculine perspective. Instead of providing us with definitive answers, Irigaray asks us to find different modes of questioning. She argues that defining or describing "women," "men," or their "sexual difference(s)" counterproductively forecloses the very social opportunities that feminists struggle to create.[1] Hence, when asked, "[W]hat is a woman?" Irigaray responds: "Can anyone, can I, elaborate another, a different, concept of femininity? There is no question of another concept of femininity. To claim that the feminine can be expressed in the form of a concept is to allow oneself to be caught up again in a system of masculine representations. . . ." (*This Sex*, 122) Similarly, she refrains from attributing specific characteristics to her vision of the future non-phallocratic "other man": "I am constantly being asked what the other man will be. Why should I appropriate for myself what that "other" man will have to say? What I want and what I'm waiting to see is what men will do and say if their sexuality releases its hold on the empire of phallocratism. But this is not for a woman to anticipate, or foresee, or prescribe. . . ." (*This Sex*, 136)

However, leaving gender-based categories open to competing historical formulations and modifications—by different social groups—is not exactly the same thing as refusing to define them altogether. Despite her claims to the contrary, Irigaray does provide us with very open "definitions"—if so they can be called—of sexual difference. In these reformulations, Irigaray accomplishes at least two interrelated objectives. First, she provides a flexible theoretical framework where masculinity and femininity function as fluid psycho-linguistic structures instead of being static definitions. These gendered structures are permeable to, and in fact inseparable from, the historical contexts and relations between men and women. Second, she engages in the pragmatic gesture of considering the social institutions and linguistic structures that enable a dialogue between men and women. Thus, Irigaray's notion of gendered intersubjectivity describes both the internalized social structures which determine the relationships among gendered individuals and, relatedly, the socio-linguistic, political, economic and cultural institutions that determine the relative power and relations between gendered communities.

By means of her multiple analogues for gendered (inter)subjectivities—the *chiasmus*, the atom, the mechanics of fluids, the *copula*, the touching lips—Irigaray delineates encounters among subjects who perceive and articulate their differences and similarities only in contact with one another and with the multiple aspects of themselves. Thus, in her analysis of Emmanuel Levinas's phenomenological ethics of alterity, which seeks to counter the Cartesian or Hegelian logic of negation or assimilation of alterity into the self-same with an unidirectional reverence of the infinite "Other," Irigaray objects (among other things) to the lack of reciprocity that defines this relation. For Levinas, the distance between "self" and "other," unlike the Hegelian relation between the ego and its projected alter ego, can never be bridged or transgressed: "If the other could be possessed, seized, and known, it would not be the other. To possess, to know, to grasp, are all synonyms of power." (*Totality and Infinity*) And yet, as

Derrida correctly points out in his generous exposition and critique of Levinas's ethics, "the Other" inevitably becomes reabsorbed into a relational comparison with the same since "[t]he infinitely other . . . can be what it is only if it is other, that is, other *than*. Other *than* must be other than myself. Henceforth, it is no longer absolved of a relation to an ego. Therefore, it is no longer infinitely, absolutely other. It is no longer what it is." (*Writing and Difference*, "Violence and Metaphysics," 1978)

Irigaray realizes both the impossibility and the undesirability of conceptualizing relations to alterity as unidirectional or non-reciprocal. This absolute separateness and distance among subjects may facilitate reverence for "the Other," but cannot create what Irigaray (along with other philosophers, including Habermas) considers to be a much needed forum for reciprocal communication. For Irigaray, the notion of reciprocity offers one of the most fruitful dimensions of intersubjective bonds. "To give, to feel . . . in return" need not depend upon the homogenization or exclusion of social differences.[2] To feel love and need love from another, to sacrifice some of your needs for another and expect that the other will also be prepared to sacrifice some of h/er, different or similar, needs for you—this ethical process is reciprocal without consuming or effacing interpersonal differences. As Irigaray states so eloquently, reciprocity can signify "I don't dominate or consume you. I respect you (as irreducible).[. . .] The "to" in her maintains the intransitivity among persons, interpellation, speech, or interpersonal gifts." (*I Love to You*, Paris: Grasset, 171–3)

"We," together yet distinct, need not keep tabs of who sacrifices more or less, "we" need not all value, share, or sacrifice the same things for one another. Quite the contrary, ethical relations depend upon incommensurable exchanges. And, as Irigaray suggests, the reciprocity of these gestures remains necessary precisely because Western societies are often based upon unreciprocal and asymmetrical relations that marginalize and devalue specific groups of people. For example, she argues that in the exchanges and "division(s) of labor" between men and women, women's exchanges have all too often taken the form of unreciprocated giving, of a gift of "self" with no return(s):

> In this possible nonsublimation of herself, and by herself, woman always tends *toward* without any return to herself as the place where something positive can be elaborated. In terms of contemporary physics, it could be said that she remains on the side of the electron, with all that this implies for her, for man, for their encounter. If there is not double desire, the positive and negative poles divide themselves between two sexes instead of establishing a *chiasmus or a double loop in which each can go toward the other and come back to itself*. If these positive and negative poles are not found in both, the same one always attracts, while the other remains in motion but lacks a "proper" place. What is missing is the double pole of attraction and support, which excludes disintegration or rejection, attraction and decomposition, but which instead ensures the separation that articulates every encounter and makes possible speech, promises, alliances. (*An Ethics*, 9)

Thus, in her ethical speculations, Irigaray wishes to reconcile the principle of incommensurability with the principle of reciprocity. How such a beautiful vision might come into being, how it could function, and what form it would take remain open and provocative questions stimulated by her models of intersubjectivity. Nevertheless, she offers us many helpful suggestions. Responding to a metaphysical heritage where "subjectivity" is conceptualized as disembodied, unchanging, masculine and univocal, Irigaray attempts reconstruct subjectivity as embodied, gendered, dialogical, dynamic, and multivocal. However, she does not completely follow those theoretical paths which conceptualize "the subject" as "a fragmentation that puts its reassemblage off to some past or future day." (*An Ethics*, 62) Instead, she articulates a permeable yet cohesive sense of "self" which remains "open into the present," "[c]losed and enveloped enough to make a self" yet "separate enough so that I can affect it and be affected by it." (*An Ethics*, 62)

If we take "uni-versality" to signify "turning toward one"—toward a masculine self-same which includes "all or a whole collectively or distributively without limit or exception"—then Irigaray's ambisexual economy cannot be labeled "uni-versal."[3] Even if we consider solely her open category of "woman," "this sex which is not one," we would not be able to identify in her theories any "essence" which pretends to depict all women under all conditions. Thus, in employing Aristotle's influential categories of "essence" versus "accident" as a litmus test for Irigaray's "essentialism," we note that Irigaray's "woman" has no one common and static "essence" (literally, 'being') which can be contrasted with other accidental properties.[4] To posit an absolute hierarchy between a primary gender-based essence and supposedly secondary attributes (such as race, class, or ethnicity) would mean to restrictively prescribe the manner in which all women should perceive themselves as well as the characteristics they should prioritize at all times: a stance which Irigaray firmly and consistently opposes. It would also directly contradict Irigaray's rigorous deconstruction of hierarchical oppositions, in which she attempts to displace the dichotomies between "a right side or a wrong side of discourse, or even of texts, [such that] each passing from one to the other would make audible and comprehensible even what resists the recto-verso structure that shores up common sense." (*This Sex*, 80) I would argue that Irigaray's reconceptualization of a (paradoxically) open category of the "universal" approximates the type of structure envisioned by Judith Butler when she calls for a "universality" which remains

> permanently open, permanently contested, permanently contingent, in order not to foreclose in advance future claims for inclusion. Indeed, from my position and from any historically constrained perspective, any totalizing concept of the universal will shut down rather than authorize the unanticipated and unanticipatable claims that will be made under the sign of "the universal." In this sense, I am not doing away with this category, but trying to relieve the category of its foundationalist weight in order to render it as a site of permanent political contest.[5]

Sexual Subjects

Unlike traditional ahistorical formulations of "universal subjectivity," both Butler's and Irigaray's reformulations acknowledge and reflect the fact that the only thing which can give meaning to the gender categories of "men" and "women" is particular individuals' identifications with, and modifications and perpetuations of these categories. In other words, for Irigaray these signifiers are dynamic, diverse, and contractual. Hence, when she argues for the necessity of diachronic identifications among multiple generations of women for the creation of a society which respects sexual difference, Irigaray depicts the "feminine" identifications among mother, daughter, and new-born girl as contractual, and even sacred, rituals: "Engendering a girl's body, bringing a third woman's body into play, would allow her to identify both herself and her mother as sexuate women's bodies. As two women, defining each other as both like and unlike, thanks to a third 'body' that both by common consent wish to be 'female.'" (*Speculum*, 35) In this description, one is both born and becomes a woman, to adapt Simone de Beauvoir's famous tenet to Irigaray's formulation of sexual difference. Although the "sexuate body" is physical or material, it is always marked by the social relations, norms and ideologies which help produce and regulate its "sexuality".

From this perspective, Diana Fuss's defense of Irigaray's "essentialism" as a strategy which attempts to ensure that under any socio-political conditions "there will always remain some part of "woman" which resists masculine imprinting and socialization" (61) risks reintroducing the dangerous supplementary paradigm of an inert, uninterpreted feminine nature (matter) formed by the active imprints of a masculine culture.[6] By situating the sexuate body "at the junction of nature and culture," (*Je, tu, nous*, 20) rather than drawing or debating their tenuous boundaries, Irigaray opens both categories for discussion and reformulation. As Judith Butler compellingly argues, instead of being automatically dismissed,

the very concept of nature needs to be rethought, for the concept of nature has a history, and the figuring of nature as the blank and lifeless page, as that which is, as it were, always already dead, is decidedly modern, linked perhaps to the emergence of technological means of domination. Indeed, some have argued that a rethinking of "nature" as a set of dynamic interrelations suits both feminist and ecological aims. This rethinking also calls into question the model of construction whereby the social unilaterally acts on the natural and invests it with its parameters and its meanings.[7]

Irigaray's theories provoke us to rethink our conceptions of ourselves, of our intersubjective bonds and antagonisms, of our histories, of our cultures. They also compel us to reconsider to what extent we can preserve, reject, or alter potentially useful—but also potentially dangerous—categories such as the "universal" versus "the particular" or "the natural" versus "the cultural." Rather than completely displacing the binary oppositions instituted by Western metaphysics, Irigaray seeks "the possibility of a different relation to the transcendental. Neither simply subjective nor simply objective, neither univocally centered nor decentered, neither unique nor plural, but as the place—up to now always collapsed in an *ek-stasis*—of what I would call the *copula*. . . ." (*An Ethics*, 153) According to Irigaray, the *ek-stasis* or the "standing out" or erection of the masculine subject needs to be replaced by the intersubjective *copula* ("is") which defines being relationally, in terms of the multiple connections among "persons of one's own and the other sex, an entire people, and people in general." (*Je, tu, nous,* 67)

Hence, we can plausibly argue that the fact that Irigaray often prioritizes changing the asymmetrical relations between men and women does not necessarily mean that she establishes a heterosexist and ethnocentric economy which, according to Kari Weil, prioritizes "the heterosexual couple as the paradigm of the ethical relationship and subordinates—indeed, elides—discussion of race, ethnicity, sexuality that cannot simply be separated from the discussion of sex and that at times must take precedence over it."[8] On the contrary, because Irigaray views subjectivity as a mode of identification (and differentiation) rather than as an essential identity, she continually stresses the necessity of a multiplicity of potential interactions among women and men. For instance, not wishing to erase, but rather to accentuate the differences among women, she explicitly cautions that "[o]ne of the dangers of love between women is the confusion of their identities, the lack of respect for or of perception of differences." (*An Ethics*, 63) In their regenerative hom(m)osexual cont(r)acts, women not only differentiate themselves from one another through communication (*parler femme*), but also collectively retrieve buried and devalorized traces of their multiple historical and spiritual genealogies that can offer them an invaluable and unprecedented sense of cultural identities.[9] In so doing, Irigaray does not equate history with mythology, thus placing information retrieval and fiction on the same epistemological plane. Instead, she suggests that any group acquires a sense of history through a re-creation and retrieval of their cultural heritage and through the continual production of cultural identities which are always being changed, challenged, and checked by new and sometimes conflicting institutional, methodological and ideological practices. While European men have had the advantage of producing this kind of dynamic sense of their histories as a group—so much so, in fact, that they have taken their histories to represent humanity as a whole—women and other historically disadvantaged groups are just beginning to create a positive sense of cultural identities.

Furthermore, since sexual identities are profoundly shaped by psycho-linguistic structures, Irigaray attempts to attenuate the sexism of language by encouraging women to "represent themselves as subjects" through articulating their gendered identities—both individually as "she-I" (*je-elle*) and collectively as "they" (*elles*)—in their interaction with one another and with men. (*Je, tu, nous,* 33–35) Hence, as the titles *Je, tu, nous* and *J'aime à toi* themselves suggest, Irigaray places the axiomatically gendered ego-structures in an intersubjective economy that permits equitable symbolic representation and exchange. By means of this relational refiguration of personal pronouns, Irigaray seeks to enrich and en-gender the ego-structures outlined by Martin Buber's correlated "I-it" (subject-object) and "I-thou" (subject-subject) relations of, respectively, domination and mutuality.[10] Retaining Buber's valuable partial collapse of the hierarchy between subject and object—where every "I-It" can become an "I-Thou" and every "I-Thou" can become an "I-it"—Irigaray places these relations within a gendered normative framework which allows both for subjective distinctness (as suggested by the accentuated diachronic separation between the *je* and the *tu* in *Je, tu, nous*) and for collective identifications among and within internally diverse groups of *nous*.

Similarly, in *J'aime à toi*, Irigaray activates a linguistic interplay of reciprocal relations which respect, without consuming or effacing, interpersonal differences. As a previously cited passage indicates, for Irigaray sexual difference implies a limitation (of each gender, race, class, etc.) that sustains a sense of respect and wonder between (always) radically different subjects: "I don't dominate or consume you. I respect you (as irreducible). [. . .] The *à* in the title maintains the intransitivity among persons, interpellation, speech or interpersonal gifts."[11] These more equitable linguistic exchanges, which enable both genders to be represented in the structures of language—as both active (transitive) and passive (intransitive), both subjects and objects, both transitive (addressed to another) and reflexive (turned toward the self)—cross the threshold (if one can be found) into Irigaray's metaphysical specul(ariz)ations of subjectivity. Conceived in this plural and dynamic fashion, "woman" can never again be identified as static and foundational, or as Irigaray states, paraphrasing Aristotle's formulation, "as place, matter, envelope for the erection of the content of civilization, its form and shaper—man." (*An Ethics*, 12)[12] In Irigaray's texts, the influential Aristotelian dichotomy between feminine matrix (inert envelope, passive matter, malleable body) and masculine form (active soul) crosses its hierarchical boundaries, reemerging as an analogue for the embodied ethical relations of gendered (inter)subjectivities.

In this process of continual self-form(ul)ation within a determined symbolic field, the subject's existence—h/er fluid boundaries, h/er changing perceptions and positions in relation to "h/erself" and "others"—depends upon revitalizing contact with differently constructed others who continually challenge and reshape h/er multiple identifications and self-definitions. This mode of self-constitution through dialogue with others resembles Bakhtin's model of dialogic subjectivity:

> I achieve self-consciousness, I become myself only by revealing myself to another, through another and with another's help. . . . Cutting oneself off, isolating oneself, closing oneself off, those are the basic reasons for loss of self. . . . It turns out that every internal experience occurs on the border, it comes across another, and this essence resides in this intense encounter. . . . The very being of man (both internal and external) is a *profound communication.*[13]

In their dialogic interactions, women and men perceive the differences and similarities which unite and separate them. Employing Bakhtin's model of dialogic communication, we could further interpret Irigaray's model of the chiasmus to entail various interactive class, race, and gender identifications and divergences that are discontinuously and diversely reinforced by particular responses to "the other(s)" rather than being essential and constant. Hence, although our symbolic order may always be coded by signifiers such as gender, race, and class, this does not necessarily mean that all subjects will be aware of these social markers in similar ways or at all times.

For example, although a white bourgeoise will always be largely affected and even formed by the symbolic field which organizes her contextual class, gender and race relations, she can occupy different subject-positions depending upon her circumstances and partners in communication. Thus, she could identify herself as a "woman" when engaged in a sympathetic dialogue with other women or in an antagonistic dialogue with men; she can be more or less aware of her socio-economic status when interacting with people of a different class; or she can be aware of her racial or ethnic differences from others when interacting with people of a different ethnicity or race. The fact that sometimes she does not foreground her identity as a woman, a white person, or a bourgeoise does not mean that she ever ceases, in Cartesian fashion, being partially determined by all of these signifiers. It does mean, however, that her agency and interactions particularize her sense of "self" and "others" in a non-negligible fashion. In other words, for Irigaray, subjectivity is constructed by a complex dialectic between a predetermined discursive field and the specific dynamic relations among and "within" embodied subjects.

Mae Gwendolyn Henderson's depiction of black women writers' representations of the dialogic modes of communication and multiple self-definitions among black women vis-à-vis black men, white women and white men provides an excellent illustration of this model of intersubjectivity:

> What is at once characteristic and suggestive about black women's writing is its interlocutory, or dialogic character, reflecting not only a relationship with the 'other(s),' but an internal dialogue with the plural aspects that constitute the matrix of black female subjectivity. [. . .] As such, black women writers enter into testimonial discourse with black men as blacks, with white women as women, and with black women as black women. At the same time, they enter into a competitive discourse with black men as women, with white women as blacks, and with white men as black women. If black women speak a discourse of racial and gendered difference in the dominant or hegemonic discursive order, they speak a discourse of racial and gender identity and difference in the subdominant discursive order. This dialogic of difference and identity characterize both black women's subjectivity and black women's discourse. It is the complexity of these simultaneous homogeneous and heterogeneous social and discursive domains out of which black women write and construct themselves (as blacks and women and, often, as poor, black women) that

enables black women writers authoritatively to speak to and engage both hegemonic and ambiguously (non)hegemonic discourse.[14]

Much as in Henderson's example, rather than erecting rigid hierarchies among various cultural markers, Irigaray's flexible ethics of intersubjectivity allows for the multiple differences among and within subjects to be manifested both individually and in their social relations. This conception of intersubjectivity, informed by an ethics of respect for oneself and for others, dissolves the boundaries between (that which has been traditionally identified as) "the contingent" and "the transcendent." Interweaving in an intricate criss-cross pattern the vertical transcendental planes of discourse relegated to the "universal" masculine subject and the horizontal immanent planes of discourse relegated to the feminine (or non-white, or non-citizen, or working class) non-subject(s), Irigaray's ethics of sexual difference enrich the signifying potential of western metaphysics and encourage the development of gendered intersubjectivity.

NOTES

1   For more discussions of Italian theories of sexual difference which rely upon the principle of social equity, see *The Lonely Mirror: Italian Perspectives on Feminist Theory*, edited by Sandra Kemp and Paola Bono. New York: Routledge, 1993.

2   Definition provided by *Webster's Ninth Collegiate Dictionary*.

3   Definition provided by *Webster's Ninth New Collegiate Dictionary*, 1291.

4   Aristotle's distinctions between essence and accident are elaborated in *Categories, Physics* (Z), and *Metaphysics*, found in McKeon 1941.

5   See Judith Butler's *Bodies That Matter: On the Discursive Limits of "Sex."* New York: Routledge, 1993. In drawing this connection I do not wish to suggest that Butler views Irigaray's reformulation of "universality" as the perfect answer to her provocative questions. Instead, I wish to argue that Irigaray provides us with a viable alternative to the choice between eliminating this category and using it in absolutist and exclusionary ways.

6   Although in *Essentially Speaking: Feminism, Nature, and Difference* (New York: Routledge, 1989), Diana Fuss sensitively reveals the potential complicity between essentialism and constructionism, in this particular passage she appears to reintroduce the binary distinctions that her project subverts.

7   Butler, 4.

8   In *Androgyny and the Denial of Difference* (Charlottesville: University of Virginia Press, 1992, 169), Kari Weil is highly sympathetic to Irigaray's ethics of sexual difference. I have chosen to cite her objections both because they are commonly raised against Irigaray's theories and because, in my opinion, Irigaray's theories can withstand these forceful critiques.

9   Irigaray's discussions of maternal genealogies can be found in *Je, tu, nous* and *Sexes and Genealogies*, trans. Gillian C. Gill. New York: Columbia University Press, 1993.

10   See *I and Thou*, trans. Ronald Gregor Smith. New York: Macmillan, 1958.

11   *J'aime à toi*, (*I Love to You*, trans. Alison Martin. New York: Routledge, 1995).

12   In *De Generatione Animalium*, Aristotle dichotomizes sexual difference as follows: "The

female always provides the material, the male that which fashions it, for this is the power that we say each possess, and this is what is meant by calling them male and female. Thus while it is necessary for the female to provide a body and a material mass, it is not necessary for the male, because it is not within the work of art or the embryo that the tools or the maker must exist. While the body is from the female, it is the soul that is from the male, for the soul is the reality of a particular body. . . ." *The Oxford Translation of Aristotle*, edited by W. D. Ross. Oxford: Clarendon Press, 1912.

13 See *The Dialogical Principle*, trans. Wlad Godzich. Minneapolis: University of Minnesota Press, 1984, 96.

14 See *Feminists Theorize the Political*, edited by Judith Butler and Joan W. Scott. New York: Routledge, 1992, 145.

chapter three

TURNING TOWARD THE UNIVERSAL

A FEMINIST CRITIQUE OF HABERMAS'S
UNIVERSALIZABILITY PRINCIPLE

The principle of "universalizability" posits that an act is judged as "ethical" only if it functions as a general "maxim" or fundamental principle that can be adopted by all "rational" agents without assuming anything specific about their (phenomenological) experiences or about their (empirical) positions and relations. This principle emerged during the age of Enlightenment under the vast, and still lasting, influence of the moral philosophy of Immanuel Kant. As Zygmunt Bauman argues in Postmodern Ethics,[1] we could describe Kant and other Enlightenment philosophers upon the universalizability of ethical principles as an effort to replace the dwindling authority of religious faith with the faith in the exercise of reason. In the late twentieth century, numerous postmodernist, poststructuralist and feminist critics have gone a long way in undermining the prerogatives of so-called "universal reason" by revealing its constitutive exclusions, hierarchies, and contradictions. Nevertheless, there remain some critics—most notably Jürgen Habermas—who find it useful to differentiate between modes of reasoning, critiquing some of its forms and reclaiming others. On the one hand, Habermas joins many other contemporary critics in questioning the effects of instrumental reason. This kind of cultural logic is oriented around the competitive accumulation of capital and the exchange and consumption of commodities in late-capitalist societies. On the other hand, Habermas wishes to perpetuate those "emancipatory" forms of critical reasoning that enable human communication—mutual understanding, critique, and conflict-resolution—among different groups and individuals.

The purpose of this essay is to critically examine Habermas's post-Enlightenment philosophy of rationalist communicative action. We will focus in particular upon his reformulation of Kant's universalizability principle and of Rousseau's notion of the general will. We will explore the following questions: By what means does the exercise of reason get correlated with moral behavior? What does the exercise of reason entail, who is best prepared to exercise it, and what exclusions and hierarchies does it depend upon? In this generally sympathetic reading of selected aspects of Habermas's works, we will be attentive not only to what Habermas borrows and modifies from Kant's and Rousseau's contractarian ethics, but also with how he remains vulnerable to—as well as indispensably helpful for—feminist critiques of "universal rationality" that have been leveled at his Enlightenment predecessors.

Moreover, by using specific feminist theories to critique the potential exclusions that the articulation of "universal reason" depends upon, I will touch upon the implications of those critiques for the feminist analyses themselves. Do feminist scholars critique the omissions and exclusions of so-called universal reason in order to render it more capacious and comprehensive a category prepared to accommodate the socio-political and cultural representation of women and other disadvantaged groups? Or, conversely, do they wish to point out the constitutive and necessary rigidity of universal reason as a "masculine" category in order to dismiss it altogether? The poles of this either-or question invoke two important approaches to feminist theory that sometimes intermingle. The first one, which both critiques and perpetuates Enlightenment rationalism, is represented by the critical theories of Seyla Benhabib and Nancy Fraser. The second, which for the most part rejects Enlightenment rationalism, is represented by Judith Butler, Chantal Mouffe, and, in some of her works, Luce Irigaray. In the first part of this essay, I will examine the notion of the general will and its application for the intersubjective communication proposed by Habermas and his sympathetic feminist critics. In the second part of the essay, I will analyze Habermas's descriptions of the subject(s) of reason interacting in the public sphere and its feminist reformulations and critiques. The objective of testing both kinds of feminist analyses against the texts of Kant, Rousseau, and Habermas is not to verify which feminist stance is most

Turning Toward the Universal

"valid" or preferable to the others, but to accentuate the usefulness, fruitful internal tensions, and sometimes telling impasses generated by feminist critiques of various models of "universal reason."

1. THE GENERAL WILL AND THE ETHICS OF INTERSUBJECTIVITY

As is well-known, for Kant, morality begins with the rejection of non-universalizable principles. Anything that cannot be adopted by all "rational" agents (whom or which we will shortly define) cannot qualify as a moral principle. This idea is formulated as the injunction, "Act only on the maxim through which you can at the same time will that it be a universal law of nature," known to us as the famous "categorical imperative."[2] As opposed to "hypothetical imperatives," that "declare a possible action to be practically necessary as a means to the attainment of something else," (82) the categorical imperative is pursued for its own sake and indicates "the ground of obligation [found] not in the nature of man nor in the circumstances in which he is placed, but solely a priori in the concept of pure reason." (57)

Like Rousseau, Kant makes the exercise of moral law dependent upon a hypothetical social contract that institutes "a systematic union of different rational beings under common laws." In this union, the sense of "duty," defined as the universalizable law that dictates how all rational men should act without taking into consideration either their personal preferences or their collective circumstances, "applies to every and all members in equal measure." (Groundwork, 100–101) Thus, for Kant the notion of morality is inextricably related to the philosopher's designation of the "rational agents" who are (by definition) exclusively qualified and authorized to exercise it. Only "rational agents" make impartial ethical decisions and treat all other rational agents (or acts) as ends rather than as means to ends. Thus, only rational agents are capable of properly ethical actions and can be regarded as equal in moral status. Because not all human beings are granted equivalent moral status (by either Kant or Rousseau), not everyone is entitled to participate in formulating or even adhering to so-called universal ethical laws, the laws of reason.

So far, the Kantian contract resembles Rousseau's "social contract." The universal principles of the social contract must remain uniform and unchangeable, "everywhere the same and everywhere tacitly admitted and recognized"[3] in order to retain ethical validity for the group of rational men it governs and binds. Both Kantian and Rousseauistic contracts are based upon presupposed (or a priori) notions of the common good. According to Kant, rational beings should be able to arrive at the same universally valid moral principles following serious critical reflection. Similarly, Rousseau posits that "[i]t is solely on the basis of this common interest that every society should be governed." (200) This common interest can be individually identified and collectively agreed upon if each person considered not his personal interests—which are presupposed to tend, "by [their] very nature, to partiality" and, through a problematic correlation, to conflict—but rather the good of all, which supposedly transcends and resolves interpersonal conflicts.

However, in developing the idea of the general will, neither Kant nor Rousseau envisions a democracy contingent upon the unanimous agreement of all of its rational members concerning the good of all. On the contrary, Kant claims that an ethical law, in order to be "valid" or universalizable, must be decided upon precisely in the absence of general deliberation. Once it becomes subject to the vicissitudes of public debates, an ethical law becomes immersed in particular interests and contingent matters and can subsequently serve, at best, only as a practical rule rather than a moral principle. Similarly, Rousseau states in an important footnote of *The Social Contract* that, "[t]o be general, a will need not always be unanimous; but every vote must be counted: any formal exclusion is a breach of generality." (201) Let us now examine some of the ramified implications and implicit assumptions behind this difference between Kantian and Rousseauistic contractarian ethics: the first (Kant's) being based solely upon a hypothetical reflection upon the common good as embodied in universalizable principles; the second (Rousseau's) being based upon a dual process that combines a hypothetical procedure and a concrete political process (voting) in the production of the general will.

Despite their shared un-democratic formulations, Kant's and Rousseau's versions of the rational-ethical contract diverge significantly concerning the notion of commensurability. Commensurability establishes the manner and criteria whereby things are assessed, compared and/or exchanged according to a common standard or measure. As we have seen, Kant's "kingdom of ends" postulates that each rational agent as well as each properly moral act are incommensurable. This means that they cannot be treated as a means to an equivalent or higher end. Conversely, Rousseau's social contract depends upon a system of exchange governed by the logic of general equivalences: "Finally, each man, in giving himself to all, gives himself to nobody; and as there is no associate over which he does not acquire the same rights as he yields others over himself, he gains an *equivalent* for everything he loses, and an increase of force for the preservation of what he has." (192)

Clearly, Rousseau's social contract is predicated upon a notion of exchange. In exchange for losing one's freedom to do harm to others in accordance with personal interests that may conflict with the "general good," a rational individual gains the protection from being harmed by others who may also act in accordance with their personal interests. In this respect, ethical principles are treated as measurable, equivalent and tradeable properties that are not necessarily good in themselves. Instead, they derive their validity from being useful to some other desired ends. Likewise, ethical agents arrive at their assessments of the general good not by immediately considering the good of all, but by assessing the personal benefits derived from considering the good of all. In many respects, Rousseau's concept of the general good, in contradistinction to Kant's, is profoundly personalized from its inception, from

Turning Toward the Universal

the mythical foundation of the social contract. We will shortly explore some of the implications of this personalized and, in many ways, egocentric Rousseauistic ethics.

Although Kant pursues a similar line of thought, for him moral law becomes operative only in contrast to, rather than as a part of, a cost-benefit analysis that belongs to a system of exchange:

> In the kingdom of ends everything has either a price or a dignity. If it has a price, something else can be put in its place as an equivalent; if it is exalted above all price and so admits no equivalent, then it has a dignity. [. . .] [T]he law-making which determines all value must for this reason have a dignity—that is, an unconditioned and incomparable worth. [. . .] Autonomy is [. . .] the ground of the dignity of human nature and of every rational nature. (*Groundwork*, 102–103)

Like Rousseau, Kant is not denying that validity-claims, including ethical propositions, must be assessed according to their value. However, as we have seen, in Rousseau's formulation value is a measurable quantity that can be exchanged in social relations and that therefore is subject to both personal and contextual evaluations. By contrast, in Kant's formulation value is an "unconditional" and "incomparable" end in itself that should be recognized as such by every rational being.

The difference between Kantian and Rousseauistic contractarian ethics stems mainly from their different premises concerning what leads individuals to bind themselves by a social contract. On the one hand, Kant assumes that rational men will have an equality of moral status that will lead them to act in accordance with universalizable principles. On the other hand, Rousseau, closer to Hobbes in this case, stresses a potential equality of physical power which makes it mutually advantageous for individuals to abide by an imaginary social contract that can reconcile their often antagonistic desires. Unlike Kant, Rousseau never assumes the infallibility of rational beings. In fact, as has been pointed out by numerous critics, he makes contradictory—and often very pessimistic—claims about "human reason." Correspondingly, he depicts the general will as dependent not only upon an *a priori* assessment of the common good on the part of each *rational* individual, but also upon a back-up collective process of deliberation that supposedly yields the general will as its mathematically calculated "remainder":

> It follows from what has gone before that the general will is always upright and always tends to the public advantage; but it does not follow that the deliberations of the people always have the same rectitude. Our will is always for our own good, but we do not always see what it is; the people is never corrupted but it is often deceived, and on such occasions only does it seem to will what is bad. There is often a great deal of difference between the will of all and the general will; the latter considers only the common interest, while the former takes private interest into account, and is no more than the sum of particular wills: but take away from these same wills the pluses and minuses that cancel one another and the general will remains as the sum of the differences. (*The Social Contract*, 203)

As we can see, Rousseau's account of the common good depends upon the establishment of a collectivity of rational beings who, much like Kant's autonomous individuals, consider only the good of all in determining their political action. However, whereas for Kant this process of abstraction is sufficient to determine proper ethical conduct, for Rousseau it is not. According to Rousseau, even rational beings who consider the good of all remain potentially swayed by particular, and thus often conflictual, interests. Thus, even rational beings can be "deceived" about the common good. When this happens, the will of all is mistaken for the general will. To correct potential errors in judgment, Rousseau institutes the general will as a concrete, not simply hypothetical, political procedure that functions in an almost mathematical fashion to (somehow) produce the right results. Since Rousseau assumes that particular interests tend to be conflictual while the general good tends to be stable, singular, and harmonious, he argues that the particular, "negative" conflicts among citizens will cancel out in the process of voting. After all is said and done, the common good, as a greatest common denominator, will remain pure and free of antagonistic claims. In turn, following the logic of the general equivalent—which needs to be removed from the market and posited as a regulative ideal in order to function as a standard for other (exchangeable) goods—the general will is itself not subject to measures or regulations. Much as Karl Marx argues concerning the general standard of gold, the general will acquires a mystified and fetishized authority.[4]

Thus, by treating human reason as fallible and contingent upon an almost mathematical political procedure to correct it, Rousseau treats rational-ethical beings—as well as their assessments of the common good—as commensurate and interchangeable. In the process of proposing the general will, each individual's truth-claim can be potentially exchanged for another's. In the last instance, all claims participate in and are measured against the resulting general will to establish, *a posteriori*, their "correctness." This contradiction, or at least tension, between Rousseau's simultaneous trust and distrust of hypothetical rational judgment leads him to establish a political economy governed by the exchange-value of collectively expressed truth-claims. One of the most problematic implications of this kind of delineation of the general will is identified by Zygmunt Bauman as he unveils the differences and the unsuspected complicities between Kant's "ends-oriented" and Rousseau's "means-oriented" contractarian ethics:

> [I]f there would be a smooth way [of] leading from many "I"s to the collective "we" only if one could posit all "I"s as by and large identical at least in respect of an attribute which assigns the units as members of one set [. . .] and therefore again in this respect, exchangeable; "we" becomes a plural of "I" only at the cost of glossing over "I's" multidimensionality. "We" is then a sum, a result of counting—an aggregate of ciphers, not an organic whole. (*Postmodern Ethics*, 47)

In the rest of this essay, we will see to what extent Habermas's formulation of communicative action is able to avoid the weaknesses, identified by Bauman and other contemporary critics, in Enlightenment contractarian ethics. More specifically, we will examine the usefulness of Habermas's communicative ethics for democratic societies which, in contradistinction to Kantian and Rousseauistic formulations, do not exclude some individuals or groups from the processes of public deliberation. As an initial step in his reformulation of the universability principle, Habermas attempts to avoid the effacement of difference into a so-called universal or neutral identity. At the same time, however, he retains the universal/rationalist criteria for negotiating among different political claims. In other words, by means of his theory of communicative action, Habermas wishes to save the best and eliminate the worst elements of Enlightenment contractarian ethics.

According to Habermas, "The concept of *communicative action* refers to the interaction of at least two subjects capable of speech and action who establish interpersonal relations (by verbal or extraverbal means). The actors seek to reach an understanding about the action situation by way of agreement. The central concept of interpretation refers in the first instance to negotiating definitions of the situation which admit of consensus." (*The Theory of Communicative Action*, vol. I, 86) Like Rousseau and Kant, Habermas tends to assume that consensus is necessary for the resolution of conflicts. He argues that a rational consensus can be reached once all (groups of) individuals—including formerly marginalized groups such as women, people of color, etc.—"express a general will" by collectively reflecting upon and disinterestedly identifying the common good. Hence, these individuals arrive at the common good only if they bracket their diverse personal interests and the differences in their social status from ethical consideration. However, at certain points, we can also interpret Habermas as stating that everything can be negotiated, including the norms and means of intersubjective debates themselves:

> Conflicts in the domain of norm-guided interactions can be traced directly to some disruption. Repairing a disrupted consensus can mean one of two things: restoring intersubjective recognition of a new validity claim after it has become controversial or assuring intersubjective recognition for a new validity claim that is a substitute for the old one. If moral argument is to produce this kind of agreement, however, it is not enough for the individual to reflect on whether he can assent to a norm. It is not even enough for each individual to reflect in this way and then to register his vote. What is needed is a "real" process of argumentation in which the individuals concerned cooperate. Only an intersubjective process of reaching understanding can produce an agreement that is reflexive in nature; only it can give the participants the knowledge that they have collectively become convinced of something.[5]

In this passage, unlike Rousseau, Habermas does not leave the identification of the general will up to the mathematical remainder that results after everyone engages in a process of hypothetical reasoning concerning the common good and subsequently registers his vote. Instead, he employs the Kantian universalizability principle from the standpoint of both the generalized (or abstract, neutral) and the concrete (or empirical) other(s) in order to arrive at some collective local understanding of the general good. If after a lengthy process of deliberation a given community does not agree upon a course of action, they can proceed with the course of action that is most endorsed by their group. During this kind of discursive process, individuals engage in,

> an intersubjective recognition of criticizable validity claims; it is thereby presupposed that those acting communicatively are *capable of mutual criticism*. But as soon as we equip the actors with this capability, we lose our privileged position as observers in relation to the object domain. We no longer have the choice of giving either a descriptive or a rational interpretation to an observed sequence of interaction. As soon as we describe *the same* judgmental competence that we claim for ourselves as interpreters of their utterances, we relinquish an immunity that was until then methodologically guaranteed. (*The Theory of Communicative Action*, vol. I, 119)

For Habermas, each individual involved in communicative action is situated within his or her community of speakers on a par with the others. This means that no person has privileged status in a given group concerning its collective decisions regardless of what social hierarchies determine their status outside of that group. This process is thus supposed to be non-hierarchical and reciprocal, in the sense that each person can contribute and critique the validity of the views expressed by other members of their community as he or she sees fit. As Habermas phrases it, all validity claims raised in the discussion can be "criticized and argued for, that is *grounded*." (*Theory of Communicative Action*, vol. I, 9) Moreover, Habermas redefines and contextualizes the notion of objectivity, which has often appeared as a privileged ahistorical position in Western metaphysics.

He argues, "A judgment can be objective if it is undertaken on the basis of a *transsubjective* validity claim that has the same meaning for observers and nonparticipants as it has for the acting subject himself." (9) This does not mean that everyone speaks from the same subject-position or shares all of the same presuppositions concerning any given claim. It does mean, however, that each individual understands that claim enough to judge it valid or invalid (defensible or indefensible) and to communicate his or her position to the other members of the group. Throughout his exposition of communicative action, Habermas relies upon the assumption that members of a given community will share some common presuppositions and linguistic habits. These shared premises—which Habermas calls the "lifeworld"—interweave the multiple and fluid fabric of intersubjective communication:

> The world gains objectivity only through counting as one and the same world for a community of speaking and acting subjects. The abstract concept of the world is a necessary condition if communicatively acting subjects are to reach understanding among themselves about what takes place in the world or is to be effected in it. Through this *communicative practice* they assure themselves at the same time of their common life-relations, of an intersubjectively shared

lifeworld. This lifeworld is bounded by the totality of interpretations presupposed by the members as background knowledge. [. . .] The conditions of validity of symbolic expressions refer to a background knowledge intersubjectively shared by the communication community. Every disagreement presents a challenge of a peculiar sort to this lifeworld background. (*The Theory of Communicative Action*, vol. I, 13)

In his writings, Habermas seems to employ the notion of the "lifeworld" in at least two distinct but interrelated ways. In the paragraph cited above, "lifeworld" offers the lowest common denominator—the cultural background and linguistic competency—necessary for collective communication. However, in his subsequent critiques of instrumental reason, he uses "lifeworld" in a broader sense by juxtaposing it to the (capitalist) "system." As Nancy Fraser encapsulates, in this case the "lifeworld" embodies "[s]ocially integrated action contexts" where "different agents coordinate their actions with one another by reference to some form of explicit or implicit intersubjective consensus about norms, values, and ends." This "consensus [is] predicated on linguistic speech and communication."[6] The "lifeworld" is continually threatened by the capitalist "system," which is based upon the ethic of profit (expropriation of surplus-value), the exploitation of the laboring classes, and the exchange and consumption of commodities—all of which are sustained by the technology/cracy of mass-media culture. Moreover, according to Habermas, the "system" disperses the public communication enabled by the lifeworld into competing interest groups. Clearly, the two definitions of the lifeworld overlap, even though, arguably, the version that is juxtaposed to the (late) capitalist "system" is more specifically historicized than the definition which is based upon speech-act and other linguistic theories.

In both cases, however, the lifeworld permits not only the critique of norms, but also the reproduction of social values and formations. As Habermas states, the lifeworld enables the "establishment of solidarity" and "the formation of personal identities." Without the lifeworld, the "*semantic* dimension of meanings or contents (of the cultural tradition), as well as in the dimensions of *social space* (of socially integrated groups), and *historical time* (of successive generations)" are severely undermined, if not altogether dissolved. (*The Theory of Communicative Action*, vol. II, 138) In other words, the lifeworld forms the cultural fabric that makes our interpellation as subjects and our identifications with others possible. Habermas declares that "the structural components of the lifeworld" are nothing less than "culture, society, person." (138) We are nevertheless led to ask how this conceptualization of the lifeworld—given its dependency upon points of contact and at least some inner harmony and coherence among and within subjects—can be plausible or useful in the context of increasingly multicultural and multiracial heterogeneous cultures. In internally diversified societies, like those found in the United States, it becomes very difficult to agree upon any shared assumptions in intra- and intercultural communication. In answer to such objections, at certain textual moments Habermas indicates that even when few premises are shared in a given social context, the very acts of interrogating and renegotiating cultural assumptions renders constructive intersubjective communication possible.

At times, Habermas himself does not hesitate to interrogate not only the "content" of knowledge and belief—doxic knowledge—but also the epistemic processes of acquiring and validating that knowledge. In his communicative ethics, everything which is not implicitly agreed upon (i.e., that which does not constitute the lifeworld) can be subject to debate and reformulation. At these times Habermas implies that being a cultural relativist, in the sense of acknowledging cultural differences, is *not* a sufficiently open position:

> The universalist position does not have to deny the pluralism and the incompatibility of historical versions of "civilized humanity"; but it regards this multiplicity of forms of life as limited to *cultural contents*, as it asserts that every culture must share certain *formal properties* of the modern understanding of the world, if it is all to attain a certain degree of "conscious awareness" or "sublimation." Thus the universalist assumption refers to a few necessary structural properties of modern life forms as such. If, however, we regard this universalist view as itself cogent only *for us*, the relativism that was rejected at the theoretical level returns at the metatheoretical level. (*The Theory of Communicative Action*, vol. I, 180)

Habermas distances himself from this latter type of universalism by critiquing both doxic and epistemic knowledge. His willingness (in this case) to negotiate not only the content, but also the means of acquiring, producing and communicating knowledge, provides an indispensable resource for feminist scholarship. Luce Irigaray, Ann Fausto Sterling, Sandra Harding, and Judith Butler (among others) have convincingly argued that what has been formerly considered as "universal" epistemic knowledge is part of the culturally variable modes of producing, categorizing and hierarchizing information that have been associated with "doxic knowledge."

In her article "Is the Subject of Science Sexed?," Luce Irigaray proposes, "In fact, what claims to be universal is the equivalent of a male idiolect, a masculine Imaginary, a sexed world—without neutrality. Unless you claim to be an unbridled defender of idealism, there is nothing surprising in this. It has always been men who have spoken and especially written, in the sciences, philosophy, religion, politics."[7] In this and other essays, she illustrates how logical discourse, the discourse conventionally deployed in argumentation and persuasion, is figuratively sexed in the masculine:

> According to the semantics of incomplete beings (Frege), functional symbols are variables found at the boundary of the identity of syntactic forms and the dominant role is given to the universality symbol or universal quantifier. The connectors are: negation, p or not p; conjunction, p or q; disjunction, p or q; implication, p implies q; equivalence, p equals q. There is no sign for difference other than quantitative, reciprocity other than within a common property or a common whole, of exchange, or permeability, of fluidity. (62)

Similarly, Irigaray points out that the rules of syntax are governed by "identity with, non-contradiction with, ambiguity, ambivalence, polyvalence minimized" and by the logic of hierarchical binary oppositions. Thus, she concludes,

> It is clear that formal language simply corresponds to the rules of the game. This language serves to define the game in such as way that a decision is possible in case of a disputed move. . . . The linguistic sciences [. . .] have not considered and even refuse at times to consider the question of the sexuality of discourse. They allow, by necessity, certain lexical terms to be added to the approved stock, new stylistic figures to impose themselves eventually, but they do not imagine that syntax and syntactic-semantic functioning are sexually-determined, and neither neutral nor universal or atemporal. (63)

While I agree with Irigaray's claim that the rules and structures of language reflect and perpetuate the social hierarchy between men and women, I would qualify that "masculine" discourse may not always be monological and that semantic structures and relations may be more unstable than Irigaray is willing to allow in this essay. As deconstructive scholarship amply illustrates, binary hierarchies simultaneously privilege and subordinate the less valued term, allowing for the subversive manipulation of its signifiers in repeated (or iterable) acts of re-interpretation or re-evaluation. Far from being a deconstructionist himself, Habermas provides us with useful modes of destabilizing binary hierarchies and of constructing—or at least envisioning—a more "egalitarian" social world.

Although in *Moral Consciousness and Communicative Action* Habermas seems to assume that in order to be able to communicate and argue with one another we need to retain the "levels of presuppositions of argumentation along the lines suggested by Aristotle: those at the logical level of products, those at the dialectical level of procedures, and those at the rhetorical level of processes," (87) at other textual moments he opens to negotiation the "masculine" presuppositions of argumentation critiqued by Irigaray. In so doing, he allows the possibility of "relocating epistemology within the terrain of modifiable social relations," as Jane Flax aptly phrases it.[8] This move enables a reconceptualization of epistemology as a discursive field of competing methods of acquiring and validating knowledge rather than as a field governed by hegemonic universal rules or ahistorical truth-claims. Seyla Benhabib pursues this paradigm shift when she states, "In the continuing and potentially unending discourse of the community of inquiry there are no "givens," there are only those aspects of consciousness and reality which at any point in time may enter into our deliberations as evidence and which we find cogent in backing our statements." (*Situating the Self*, 5) Once everything can be subject to debate within a given context—including "the rules of the game" themselves—the constraint of neutrality will no longer prevent those groups who have been previously marginalized from both cultural and political representation from articulating their diverse concerns, interests, and perspectives.

However, their marginalization cannot be corrected by simply adding, for example, women, members of the working class individuals or people of color to the old universal picture. The gesture of "pluralist" inclusion, in itself, is not likely to change the rules of the game since, as Benhabib notes, the exclusions constituted "not just a political omission and a moral blind spot but [. . .] an epistemological deficit as well." (*Situating the Self*, 12–13) Making epistemic as well as doxic knowledge subject to intersubjective debates does not refer to the production of what Jane Flax justifiably criticizes as "standpoint epistemologies" that "entail the assumption that there is a relatively stable, similarly determined unit of experience that can and should be represented through a single category." (*Disputed Subjects*, 23) To merely present knowledge from a "woman's point of view," or an "African-American perspective" would repeat the universalist gesture of homogenizing and essentializing internally diverse groups of people. Instead, Flax argues that we need to envision a political forum where social identifications are acknowledged as "constituted by complex, overdetermined, and multiple processes [that] are historically variable and internally contradictory." (23) In other words, she proposes a public sphere where affiliations can be formed and disagreements can be expressed. In order to outline this relatively open and dynamic public sphere, we will turn to Habermas's reformulation of the Kantian and Rousseauistic versions of the public sphere delineated in his early work *The Structural Transformation of the Bourgeois Public Sphere*. Our analysis will be closely guided by Nancy Fraser's important feminist critique of Habermas's project, undertaken in her essay, "Rethinking the Public Sphere: A Contribution to the Critique of Actually Existing Democracy."[9]

2. THE MAN OF REASON AND DEBATES IN THE PUBLIC SPHERE

In the essay "What is Enlightenment?" Kant argues that man's "public use of [his] reason undirected by "external" forces,

> must always be free and it alone can bring about enlightenment among men. The private use of reason, on the other hand, may often be very narrowly restricted without particularly hindering the progress of enlightenment. By the public use of one's reason I understand the use which a person makes of it as a scholar before the reading public. Private use I call that which one may make of it in a particular civil post or office entrusted to him. [. . .] But so far as a part of the mechanism regards himself as a member of the whole community or of a society of world citizens, and thus in the role of a scholar who addresses the public [. . .] through his writings, he can argue [and criticize] without hurting the affairs for which he is in part responsible as a passive member. (*Collected Works*, 265)

As Jane Flax explains in *Disputed Subjects*, Kant establishes two sets of dichotomies between "private/passive" and "public/both active and passive" exercises of reason. The first one, associated with the "passive" feminine private sphere as opposed to the potentially "active" masculine public sphere, deploys the metaphors of the child's mental and physical dependence (or "tutelage") upon his mother. Kant argues that men must learn to overcome this dependency—one that binds children for part of their lives and "the entire fair sex" for their whole lives—by "falling a few times [and then] learning to walk alone." Rather than valorizing the interconnectedness and interdependency symbolized by domestic relations, Kant privileges the individuation and autonomy that men develop in public interaction.[10]

Kant's second articulation of the public-active/private-passive dichotomy occurs within the fold of the masculine public sphere itself. Here he juxtaposes the public-active or emancipatory reason exercised by a few autonomous producers of knowledge like himself with the private-passive instrumental reason that all citizens use in obeying civil laws. In this public sphere, both the public-active and the private-passive uses of reason are functions exercised by men in their dual social status as obedient citizens and critical producers of laws. Certainly the role which Kant calls "private-passive" is presented as far less valuable than the public-active, critical, and emancipatory role exercised by the citizen-scholar. Not surprisingly, this "private-passive" role also carries inevitable gendered connotations with the less valued "feminine" private sphere.

Women, unpropertied men, and non-whites are, for circular reasons, automatically disqualified by Kant from participating in the "active" masculine public sphere of emancipatory reasoning. Without women's exclusion from the political domain, it appears that the gender-sex system would be severely unsettled. Both Kant and Rousseau insist upon the complementarity of gender roles by predicating masculinity upon a rational critical reflection about and participation in culture and politics from which women are normatively excluded. Although these Enlightenment philosophers had benefited from the reception of intellectual women in their literary salons who spread their fame and scholarship, they proceeded to compartmentalize gender roles according to hierarchical distinctions between masculine and feminine "economies." Rousseau, for example, notoriously claims, "A female wit is a scourge to her husband, her children, her friends, her servants, to everybody. From the lofty height of her genius, she scorns every womanly duty, and she is always trying to make a man of herself . . . ." (*Emile*). Without women remaining both different and—despite the philosophers' claims to equivalence and complementarity—subordinate, the privileged masculine positions become threatened out of cultural dominance, if not out of existence.

Thus, in *Observations on the Feeling of the Beautiful and Sublime*,[11] Kant addresses his implied readers, whom he apparently assumes to be, and encodes as, "male":

> I hope the reader will spare me the reckoning of the manly qualities, so far as they are parallel
> to the feminine, and be content only to consider both in comparison to the other. The fair sex has
> just as much understanding as the male, but it is a beautiful understanding, whereas ours should

be a deep understanding, an expression that signifies identity with the sublime. [. . .] Deep med-
itation and long-sustained reflection are noble but difficult, and do not well befit a person in
whom unconstrained charms should show nothing else than a beautiful nature. Laborious learning or painful pondering, even if a woman should greatly succeed in it, destroy the merits that
are proper to her sex, and because of their rarity they can make of her an object of cold admira-
tion; but at the same time they will weaken the charms with which she exercises her great power
over the other sex. (78)

The shifting authorial and reader gender constructs encoded in this text are very
telling. Kant initially appears to privilege "the fair sex" in the binary dichotomy of feminine and masculine economies. He claims that he is not concerned with "the
masculine" side of the equation. It suffices to delineate "the feminine," and "the masculine" will be implicitly understood as "parallel" or complementary to the feminine.
Nevertheless, by this very focus upon "the feminine," Kant encloses the feminine functions he relegates to women within a textual field already marked as "masculine."
Rhetorically, he addresses a universalized male audience, an "us" who presumably
agree upon the divisions established between "our" (men's) deep sublime understanding and "their" (women's) surface complementary and subordinate beautiful
understanding. This implied universal "male" audience, the audience of impartiality,
will comprehend and accept the ambivalent gesture of respect and condescension with
which the implied [male] author at once flatters and dismisses women as both too
charming and too frivolous to engage in what he (reflexively) considers deep thought.
Male readers who do not participate in this universal audience are only nominally
included in this conversation predicated upon agreement.[12] Their addition to the collective discussion functions as a "dangerous supplement" that threatens to displace
the unity of the masculine universal audience implied by the text.

The women who read and disagree with Kant's text threaten its terms and binary
hierarchies perhaps even more so than those readers marked as "men." If reading
within the prescriptive boundaries articulated by the text, they can only function
to sustain Kant's argument. By means of participating as readers in this discussion
between (implied) men, female readers are the bad exceptions that proves the rule.
How can those readers who are culturally marked as "women" participate in a
homosocial conversation among men and about women? As Eve Sedgwick insight-
fully points out, through "the presence of a woman who can be seen as pitiable and
contemptible, men are able to exchange power and to confirm each other's value
even in the context of the remaining inequalities of their power."[13] To say no as a
male reader, to read "as a woman," is to read Kant's text against its grain.

But perhaps if one takes Kant at his word, Kant's words should be read critically,
if not subversively. This would involve questioning the gender-sex system he proposes. First of all, we can dispute Kant's reduction of women to a means to an end,
a point of contention that accepts Kantian ethics and critiques it from within. More

radically and perhaps more effectively, we can disrupt the gender hierarchy he proposes by interrogating and displacing its terms. To some extent Kant's text provides feminist readers with the tools of such a critical subversion. So far, I have argued that he assumes a universal male audience, preferably one that agrees with his gender-sex system. However, if Kant were only addressing a male audience that he hoped to persuade, then why does he repeatedly go through the motions of appearing to valorize feminine roles as equivalent to male ones? As we remember, on numerous occasions he emphasizes that "the fair sex has just as much understanding as the male." Is Kant's text not engaging in a performative contradiction? Or at the very least, is it not enacting the logic of "that dangerous supplement" by explicitly marginalizing but implicitly targeting, or centralizing, "female" readers? These strategies of soliciting the complicity of the marginalized in the very act of their marginalization, strategies that continually surface in Kant's writing, can be seen as a symptom of a larger cultural phenomena that make devalorized groups of people complicit in the norms that—at least in the case of women—seductively subordinate them.

I believe that the subversion of these universalist rhetorical strategies begins with the textual inscription of those obliquely hailed by Kant's text as marginal yet also central—"women." This inscription, which will position women on the margins—at the externalized interior or internalized exterior—of Kant's homosocial discourse will function as what Trinh T. Minh-ha eloquently calls ". . . our sites of survival, [. . .] our fighting grounds and their site for pilgrimage," that enable "a certain work of displacement [whereby] strategies of reversal [. . .] meet their own limits." (*When the Moon Waxes Red*) Only by confronting and challenging these limits can we, the partial readers interpellated (and resisting interpellation) by universalist texts, construct a world in which even gender-marked terms can acquire emancipatory meanings.

By contrast, reading Kant's text without challenging its hierarchies, blindspots and exclusions, cannot yield emancipatory interpretations. Since without political participation, women cannot develop the rational capacities that Kant considers necessary for the formation of moral character—precisely because moral character depends upon political autonomy—this lack of moral disposition in turn (by a circular reasoning) disqualifies them from inclusion in the public sphere. Of course, Kant admits that women, though educationally and naturally the complements or supplements of men, could develop the rational capacities necessary for the exercise of autonomous judgment. Nevertheless, as we have seen, he vehemently argues against the education of women's "rational abilities." As Bauman suggests, Kant, like other Enlightenment political philosophers, bases his claims upon confused but strategically self-empowering premises concerning the relations between nature and culture:

> At no time were the philosophers prominent for high regard for 'empirical' men and women. This presented them with a problem, and a difficult one—since it was on the 'nature' of such men and women that they sought to found the ethical code which was in its turn to legitimize the role

of the enlighteners as ethical legislators and moral guardians. There was just one conceivable solution to the quandary: yes, it is the nature of man that will provide a rock-solid, and sufficient foundation for the universally binding ethical code; but no, it is not the 'nature of men and women' as it stands at the moment, as it can be seen and recorded today, that will serve as such a foundation. This is so because what we can see and report now is not the manifestation of 'true human nature'. Nowhere yet has human nature been properly fulfilled. Human nature exists at present solely *in potentia*; as a possibility not-yet-born, awaiting a [philosopher] midwife to let it out, and not before a protracted labor and acute birth-pangs. . . . Two things had to be done first for that potential to turn into daily reality of life. First, the moral potential hidden in human beings should be revealed to them; people had to be enlightened as to the standards they were able to meet but unable to discover unaided. And second, they had to be helped in following such standards by an environment carefully designed to favor and reward genuinely moral conduct. Both tasks evidently required professional skills—first of [philosopher-]teachers, then of legislators. (Postmodern Ethics, 26–27)

Rousseau claims, "Man is born free and everywhere he is in chains," and promises to show "us" how to free "ourselves": that is, if "we" belong to a select group of privileged men. Similarly, Kant promises to illuminate the path to a similarly restricted group's enlightenment: "If we were asked, 'Do we now live in an enlightened age?' the answer is 'No,' but we live in an age of enlightenment.' As things now stand, much is lacking which prevents men from being, or easily becoming, capable of correctly using their own reason [. . .] with assurance and free from outside direction." (*What is Enlightenment*, 267–68) Since strictly prescribing the behavior of white and relatively wealthy male citizens might hamper their autonomy, the most convenient way of changing men consists in prescribing and confining the role of those marked as their cultural subordinates: namely, of women.

For example, eliding the distinction between women's "nature" and their gender-specific education and between what women do and what women should do, Kant urges women to experience "[n]ever a cold and speculative instruction but always feelings, and those indeed which remain as close as possible to the situation of her sex. . . . Nothing of duty, nothing of compulsion, nothing of obligation! Woman is intolerant of all commands and all morose constraint. . . . But in the place of it Providence has put in her breast kind and benevolent sensations, a fine feeling for propriety, and a complaisant soul." (81) He maintains that a rigorous education would "weaken the charms with which she exercises her great power over the other sex." (81) In other words, contrary to his own ethical theory that prohibits the treatment of human beings as a means to an end rather than as ends-in-themselves, Kant argues that patriarchal society should discourage women from exercising moral reasoning in order to continue to treat women as a means to the rational and moral development of a few empowered men. It is significant to note that Kant's formulation of the "kingdom of ends" argument only applies to rational beings: "For rational beings all stand under the law that each of them should treat himself and all others, never merely as a means, but always at the same time as an end in himself." (*Groundwork*, 101) Thus the laws binding the ethical conduct of rational beings only apply to other rational beings: autonomous men are forbidden from treating other autonomous men solely as a means to an end, no matter how valuable that end may be.

However, in the case of those liminal beings who are defined as only ambiguously rational—like women and people of color—the terms of the pact are not binding in the same fashion. Kant nowhere forbids treating non-rational beings solely as a means to higher ends. Following the supplementary logic traced by Derrida in Rousseau's works, Kant's definition of so-called autonomous men is wholly dependent upon the nurturing—but also potentially disruptive—roles of definitionally less rational women. Hence, rather than excluding "personal" considerations from moral judgment, as his theory of "transcendental apperception"[14] postulates, Kant makes moral judgment dependent upon "personal" status. This status includes the subject's gender (male), race (white), and class position (middle or upper class). Only once these criteria have been factored in, can other personal matters, like emotions, preferences, desires and tastes, be factored out.

Can Habermas modify the Kantian principle of universalizability in a manner that would democratically include the groups it originally marginalized? In order to begin answering this question we must take a look at Habermas's redefinition of reason:

> When we use the expression 'rational' we suppose that there is a close relation between rationality and knowledge. Our knowledge has a propositional structure; beliefs can be represented in the form of statements. I shall presuppose this concept of knowledge without further clarification, for rationality has less to do with the possession of knowledge than with how speaking and acting subjects *acquire and use knowledge.* [. . .] If we seek the grammatical subjects that go with the predicate expression 'rational,' two candidates come to the fore: persons, who have knowledge, can be more or less rational, as can symbolic expressions—linguistic and nonlinguistic, communicative or noncommunicative actions—that embody knowledge. We can call men and women, children and adults, ministers and bus conductors 'rational,' but not animals or lilac bushes, mountains, streets, or chairs. (*The Theory of Communicative Action*, vol. I, 8)

Clearly, in Habermas's reformulation, reason becomes a cognitive capacity, minimally defined as the ability to acquire, use, and communicate knowledge, shared by all human beings. In order to analyze how and where rational beings can exercise their reasoning capacities according to Habermas's paradigm, I would like to turn to Nancy Fraser's exposition and critique of Habermas's description of the bourgeois public sphere.

In her essay "Rethinking the Public Sphere: A Contribution to the Critique of Actually Existing Democracy," Fraser confronts Habermas's unitary notion of the (single) bourgeois public sphere with critical narratives provided by revisionist his-toriography. By the end of her fruitful juxtaposition, we are left neither with Habermas's idealization of unity, nor with the revisionist historiographers' disper-sion of Habermas's potentially useful forum for public communication. Instead, we perceive the possibility of a multiplicity of discursive forums and formations that allow for and even strengthen the expression of diverse points of view.

Fraser begins her critical reformulation of Habermas's bourgeois public sphere by introducing Habermas's presentation of it in his doctoral thesis, *The Structural Transformation of the Public Sphere: An Inquiry into a Category of Bourgeois Society.* She explains that Habermas situates the bourgeois public sphere as a forum that emerged during the seventeenth and eighteenth centuries, where middle-class men would critique the cultural and, later, the political practices of (Western European) absolutist regimes. This forum provided "a theater in modern societies in which political par-ticipation is enacted through the medium of talk." (*Unruly Practices*, 110) Such talk served an important double function. First of all, it provided a "public" arena where "private" citizens could be dialogically critical of the state. Second, it also provided a space which could be distinct from and critical of dominant economic relations. In other words, for Habermas the bourgeois public sphere came into being as an emancipatory site of enlightened critical distance from the dominant political regimes and economic forces governing modern Western European society.

It is worth noting, however, that even this initial proposition is persuasively con-tested by subsequent historical research. For example, Terry Eagleton (in *Criticism and Ideology, The Function of Criticism*) and Tony Bennett (in *Outside Literature*) have argued that rather than assuming a primarily critical function, the members of the bourgeois public sphere fostered alliances between themselves and the aristocracy in an attempt to dissolve "the [class] distinction between bourgeois, squire, artistocrat and the members of the professions in involving them in the same institutions as co-dis-covering equals." (*Outside Literature*, 227) However, whether or not the bourgeois public sphere satisfactorily engaged in its alleged critical functions, Habermas main-tains that such functions should be its role. He is particularly concerned with what he considers to be a decline and dispersion of the public sphere in late-capitalist soci-eties. In such societies, state and public bureaucracies and big businesses minutely regulate both the "private" and the (small-business) economic sector. In addition, they are taking control of all of the important public functions, including education and the mass media. According to Habermas, this kind of technocratic infiltration leaves very little space for autonomous and critical cultural activity.

While Fraser agrees with Habermas about the necessity of this critical forum of collective deliberation, she begins to distance herself from his increasing emphasis upon the unity of the public sphere that engages citizens in a Rousseauistic search for their "common interest." Her own description of Habermas's project dramatizes its abrupt transition between a collective political critique, which in principle can accommodate a multiplicity of agents, interests, and points of view, to a collective focus upon deliberating, identifying and representing the so-called "common interest" of "bourgeois society":

> These publics aimed to mediate between society and the state by holding the state accountable to society via publicity. At first this meant requiring that information about state functioning be made accessible so that state activities would be subject to critical scrutiny and the force of public opinion. Later it meant transmitting the considered "general interest" of "bourgeois society" to the state via forms of legally guaranteed free speech, free press, and free assembly, and eventually through the parliamentary institutions of representative government. (112)

Some of the immediate questions provoked by Habermas's rough transition from collective critique to collective agreement are the following. What is the "general interest," how did the bourgeois interest come to be identified as general, and why should it be sought? We could also ask in what ways is this general interest inclusive, and what and whom it includes. Furthermore, we are led to wonder in what ways the political consolidation of this "general interest" depends upon the exclusion of those agents and groups who are not likely to share the "general interest" of "bourgeois society." As formulated, these questions combine two sets of interrelated concerns that are addressed by Fraser throughout her article. First, given (necessarily) less than ideal historical conditions, is consensus a viable option? Second, even given ideal historical conditions that would allow all people to voice their concerns in a fair and "egalitarian" fashion, is *unity*—in the form of deliberating within a *single* public sphere, of finding a *common* interest, and of reaching *consensus*—a desirable political objective? Rather than grouping together these (separate but interrelated) empirical and normative questions, Fraser chooses to turn first to history in order to address the problems posed by theory. If, by means of historical analysis, she can demonstrate that the seemingly inclusive project of determining a common social interest necessarily depends upon various exclusions and marginalizations, then she can seriously undermine—though she does not intend to completely refute—Habermas's theoretical project of reaching universal consensus through dialogic communication in a single public sphere.

The historiographic accounts presented by Joan Landes, Mary Ryan, and Geoff Eley explicitly describe the political exclusions from the bourgeois public sphere which Habermas's narrative leaves implicit. As Fraser suggests,

> For Landes, the key axis of exclusion is gender; she argues that the ethos of the new republican public sphere in France was constructed in deliberate opposition to that of a more woman-friendly salon culture that the republicans stigmatized as "artificial," "effeminate," and "aristocratic." Consequently, a new, austere style of public speech and behavior was promoted, a style deemed "rational," "virtuous" and "manly." (115)

Similarly, Geoff Eley illustrates that the "bourgeois public sphere" remained, in fact, "bourgeois" not only in its historical formation but also in its socio-economic constitution and class-based interests. In other words, it excluded working-class people from political participation by means of a combination of formal and informal impediments. These historical revisions cast doubt upon Habermas's theoretical project. They reveal not only that the "bourgeois public sphere" was far from egalitarian—a fact which Habermas already concedes—but also suggest that the idea(l) of a universal sphere for the formation of a "general interest" depends upon, to use Kristeva's term, a process of "abjection." This process describes the mechanisms of power by which dominant groups, ideological structures, or individuals produce the effect of an idealized unity (an inside or a core) through the exclusion of a potential diversity that is represented as undesirable (or abject). According to Fraser, the fact that all women and most men were represented as "different" or "other" and excluded from the bourgeois public sphere was not merely a historical accident. On the contrary, it was a necessary result of the theoretical idealization of unity and repudiation of diversity, be it in terms of forum(s) of discussion, expression of social interest(s), or reaching (or failing to reach) agreement following public deliberations.

In her powerful critique, Fraser employs "revisionist historiography" to systematically attack each modality of unity posited as desirable by Habermas's version of the bourgeois public sphere. She begins by illustrating that the notion of a unified and fair collective participation depends upon certain exclusions of dissimilar political agents or groups who might jeopardize the project of reaching consensus. Analogously, she proceeds to show that the notion of a single public sphere is also not all-inclusive (as Habermas postulates) but depends upon the exclusion of

> other, nonliberal, nonbourgeois, competing public spheres. [. . .] Ryan's study shows that even in the absence of formal political incorporation through suffrage, there were a variety of ways of accessing public life and a multiplicity of public arenas. Thus the view that women were excluded from the public sphere turns out to be ideological; it rests on a class- and gender-biased notion of publicity, one which accepts at face value the bourgeois public's claim to be the public. In fact, the historiography of Ryan and others demonstrates that the bourgeois public was never *the* public. On the contrary, virtually contemporaneous with the bourgeois public sphere arose a host of competing counterpublics, including nationalist publics, popular peasant publics, elite women's publics, and working-class publics. Thus there were competing publics from the start, not just in the late nineteenth and twentieth centuries, as Habermas implies. (115)

Once again with the help of revisionist historiography, Fraser illustrates that past historical "realities" have present theoretical implications for Habermas's model of the public sphere. Habermas neither proves that there is a single public sphere, nor assumes that there was a single, self-conscious and unified forum for political critique and discussion. These assumptions, though certainly problematic and vulnerable to historical counterfactuals and to theoretical challenges, would nevertheless enable him to posit that unity is both possible and desirable. For if we accept that the only possible critical forum is concentrated within a single public sphere, then it follows that this kind of public sphere does not depend upon the exclusion of other public spheres. However, as suggested, this is not what Habermas claims. Rather than assuming "the bourgeois public sphere" to be the only public sphere, Habermas assumes it to be the central and most effective forum for critical political deliberation. In other words, he leaves himself open to the objections that by focusing upon and centralizing this sphere at the expense of other political spheres, his theoretical project not merely represents but actually reinforces the historical gesture that marginalized other public spheres.

As Martha Nussbaum suggests in a different context, even conceptually—not to speak of pragmatically—an emphasis upon unity and consensus can seriously undermine, if not preclude, a respect for differences: "[. . .]we might infer that to do justice to the nature or identity of two distinct values requires doing justice to their difference—both their qualitative distinctness and their numerical separateness—requires seeing that there are, at least potentially, circumstances in which the two will collide. Distinctness requires articulation from, bounding off against. This, in turn, entails the possibility of opposition—and, for the agent who is committed to both—of conflict." (*The Fragility of Goodness*, 68) Although Habermas allows for inclusive "membership" and open-ended debates within the public sphere, his emphasis upon a single sphere—in a society where distinct spheres could exist—and upon eventual agreement considerably weakens his expressed concern for difference.

Fraser's next, and related, point of inquiry focuses upon Habermas's ideal of political consensus among or within (the) public sphere(s). According to revisionist historiography,

> not only were there always a plurality of competing publics, but the relations between bourgeois publics and other publics were always conflictual. Virtually from the beginning, counterpublics contested the exclusionary norms of the bourgeois public, elaborating alternative styles of political behavior and alternative norms of public speech. Bourgeois publics in turn excoriated these alternatives and deliberately sought to block broader participation. (116)

While Fraser distances herself from any unqualified postulation of perpetual conflict between the bourgeois public sphere and the other public spheres, she allows for the possibility of both conflict and potential aggreements among public spheres. As previously suggested, since Habermas's account glosses over (without denying) the existence of alternative public spheres, he consequently fails to consider their relations to the bourgeois public sphere that he uncritically centralizes. But this does not mean that he assumes that these potential alternative spheres are in harmonious—or for that matter conflictual—relations to the dominant bourgeois public sphere.

This blind spot in Habermas's narrative enables revisionist historiographers to introduce their own accounts of conflictual relations, accounts which need to be taken into consideration. For if there are fundamental points of tension and diversity of interests among public spheres, then how is an emphasis upon unity conceptually prepared to address these problems?

Although he does not confront these objections explicitly, Habermas relies upon certain assumptions that address them implicitly. As Fraser goes on to explain, "Habermas's account of the bourgeois conception of the public sphere stresses its claim to be open and accessible to all. Indeed, this idea of open access is one of the central meanings of the norm of publicity." (118) In Habermas's view, the central bourgeois public sphere could accommodate both already existing and forming alternative public spheres. That is, it included, or could include, them in its own capacious and open forum for public discussion. No issues, even those which may cause tension, need be declared off-limits. The function of a bourgeois public forum is precisely to come to terms with social agreements and disagreements as long as the discussion eventually reaches some type of "rational" consensus. Nevertheless, without providing sufficient justification, Habermas seems to assume that the bourgeois public sphere would be willing and able to incorporate competing group interests. Conversely, he also assumes that competing groups would be willing and able to participate in the bourgeois public sphere. What Fraser wishes to suggest is that such highly optimistic assumptions cannot be either practically or theoretically granted. In so far as diversity of background, interest, and opinion among individuals and groups can be assumed to exist in a democratic society, the possibility of collective affinities and of *irreconcilable* tensions cannot be ignored. On the contrary, such possibilities must be addressed by any viable model of communicative political theory.

In all fairness we must add that in most of his later works, Habermas takes into consideration diversity and disagreement much more seriously. For example, in *Moral Consciousness and Communicative Action*, he acknowledges that agreement is often obtained by means of force of arms or words rather than persuasion: "Like all argumentation, practical discourses resemble islands threatened with inundation in a sea of practice where the pattern of consentual conflict resolution is by no means the dominant one. The means of reaching agreement are repeatedly thrust aside by the instruments of force. [. . .] These limitations of practical discourses testify to the power history has over transcending claims and interests of reason." (106) Indeed, as Judith Butler points out in *Gender Trouble*, what constitutes agreement for one party may mean coercion for another, and the notions of "agreement," "dialogue," and the discursive practices and power relations that enable or prevent them need themselves to become a part of the collective deliberations. Although Habermas acknowledges that members of a community can sometimes fail to reach agreement ("Both attempts can fail; the consensus sought can fail to come to pass, the desired

Turning Toward the Universal

effect can fail to take place") his theory does not elaborate modes of resolving these impasses and conflicts. (*The Theory of Communicative Action*, vol. I, 11)

In so far as the emphasis remains on the resolution of conflicts to reach consensus, on both counts, "practical" and "theoretical," Habermas's theory is unprepared to deal with inevitable social conflicts. Fraser reminds us that, from a historical point of view, "[t]he question of open access cannot be reduced without remainder to the presence or absence of formal exclusions. It requires us to look at the process of discursive interaction within formally inclusive public arenas " while "informal impediments to participatory parity [. . .] can persist even after everyone is formally and legally licensed to participate." (118–119) Moreover, from a conceptual point of view, Fraser asks us to remember that Habermas's version of "the bourgeois public sphere requires *bracketing* inequalities of status." (118)

It is worth examining what exactly Habermas means by requiring citizens to "bracket" their differences upon entering the bourgeois public sphere. Is he requiring people to set aside, erase, ignore or merely not centralize their socio-political differences? Significantly, Habermas borrows the term from the transcendental phenomenology of Edmund Husserl. Following Descartes's sceptical method of ontological doubt, which excludes all experiences that cannot be substantiated "clearly and distinctly" as proof of one's existence until one arrives at the mental certainty of one's ability to think, Husserl uses the term to focus attention upon the discoveries of the mind by bracketing the "external" world ascertained through (the supposedly more fallible) sense-perceptions. According to Husserl, after being bracketed, our impression of the external world "undergoes a modification—while remaining in itself what it is, we set it as it were 'out of action,' we 'disconnect it,' 'bracket it.' It still remains there like the bracketed in the bracket, like the disconnected outside the connexional system." (*Ideas*, 98) Thus, through the process of bracketing we neither ignore nor efface a phenomenon. Instead, we effectively marginalize it by disconnecting it from the targeted subject under consideration. Habermas himself engages in the process of bracketing when he presents the following narrative about the development of the bourgeois public sphere:

> First they [coffeehouses, salons, and other sites of the public sphere] preserved a kind of social intercourse that, far from presupposing the equality of status, disregarded status altogether. The tendency replaced the celebration of rank with a tact befitting equals. The parity on whose basis alone the authority of the better argument could assert itself against that of social hierarchy and in the end can carry the day meant, in the thought of the day, the parity of "common humanity" ("*bloss Menschliche*"). *Les hommes*, private gentlemen, or *die Privatleute* made up the public not just in the sense that power and prestige of public office were held in suspense; economic dependencies also in principle had no influence. Laws of the market were suspended as were laws of the state. [. . .] If not realized, [equality] [. . .] was at least consequential. (*Structural Transformation of the Bourgeois Public Sphere*, 36)

In considering this proposition, we will analyze what specifically Habermas wishes to bracket. Then we will interrogate the desirability of the process of bracketing. Habermas begins his narrative by claiming that the bourgeois public sphere was a place where inequality of status was acknowledged but regarded as unimportant as a matter of etiquette, with a "tact befitting equals." While seeming to address different types of (often intersecting) social asymmetries, Habermas actually deals with only one specific case of it. He focuses upon class-based inequality, which he labels "inequality of status." It seems that here he adopts a Weberian definition of class—one based upon socio-economic distinctions between groups—rather than a Marxian definition, based upon the ownership of the relations of production.[15] It is worth noting that there are a number of asymmetrical power relations which Habermas does not even mention. Gender, racial, ethnic, and national hierarchies, though as relevant as class hierarchies, seem to be not only bracketed, but entirely absent from Habermas's narrative of the bourgeois public sphere.

By the end of the passage cited above, Habermas once again rhetorically duplicates women's exclusion from the public sphere. He celebrates the so-called equality of citizens consisting of "*bloss Menschliche,*" [the simply human] "*les hommes,*" and "private gentlemen," all of whom are seemingly inclusive but actually masculine signifiers that both reflect and enact the exclusion of women from the public sphere. The only term used by Habermas which signifies both men and women is *die Privatleute,* or the private people, whose historical referent happened to be—once again—only men.

If, along with Nancy Fraser, we were to include gender, race, sexual orientation and any other group-formations, which provide both a target for systematic group-based discrimination as well as a site of group-based affiliations and divisions, as indices of systematic power asymmetries, then the process of "bracketing" social differences would no longer appear as our optimal practical or theoretical option. Fraser persuasively argues,

> Insofar as the bracketing of social inequalities in deliberation means proceeding as if they did not exist when they do, this does not foster participatory parity. On the contrary, such bracketing usually works to the advantage of dominant groups in society and to the disadvantage of subordinates. In most cases it would be more appropriate to unbracket inequalities in the sense of explicitly thematizing them—a point that accords with the spirit of Habermas's later communicative ethics. (120)

Once again we turn away from a universal suspension of group differences to their explicit articulation in public deliberations which acknowledge the partiality of each rather than insisting upon the universal rational agreement of all. "Minoritary" group formations provide the forums where social views are formed, shared, and articulated in a manner that renders their expression—be it consonant or dissonant with respect to dominant ideologies and practices—more forceful and effective. For example, Fraser suggests that such alternative public forums are especially helpful for formulating and articulating the interests of marginalized groups like women or people of discriminated races and ethnicities whose multiple "perspectives" may not have had the chance to be developed through coalitional politics and have been effectively bracketed from the bourgeois public sphere. Fraser proposes to call these marginalized public spheres "subaltern counterpublics" in order to signal that they are "parallel discursive arenas where members of subordinated social groups invent and circulate counterdiscourses to formulate oppositional interpretations of their identities, interests, and needs." (122) It seems to me that at this point Fraser partially duplicates Habermas's troublesome emphasis upon political unity. Not only is she granting Habermas's version of "the bourgeois public sphere" a questionable cohesion that elsewhere she continually challenges and undermines, but also she seems to rely upon a unified conception of the identity-based coalitions formed within various "subaltern counterpublics." Neither model seems adequate to her task, which involves the political expression of diverse as well as similar interests and points of view. As Judith Butler suggests,

> Perhaps a coalition needs to acknowledge its contradictions and take action with those contradictions intact. Perhaps also part of what dialogic understanding entails is the acceptance of divergence, breakage, splinter and fragmentation as part of the often tortuous process of democratization. The very notion of "dialogue" is culturally specific and historically bound and while one speaker may feel secure that a conversation is happening, another may be sure it is not. [. . .] The assumption of [an identity-based coalition's] essential incompleteness permits that category to serve as a permanently available site of contested meanings. The definitional incompleteness of the category might then serve as a normative ideal relieved of coercive forces. (*Gender Trouble*, 15)

According to Butler, a coalition does not have to involve presupposing or even establishing through collective deliberation points of similarity alone. Her version of public spheres—if they can be called so—is local, permeable, and dynamic, leaving open discursive practices and paradigms of subjectivity that, to use Jane Flax's fitting depiction, are "fluid rather than solid, contextual rather than universal, and process-oriented rather than topographical." (*Disputed Subjects*, 93) Contrary to what some critics of postmodern ethics may claim, the heterogeneity and overdetermination of subject-positions does not necessarily entail the complete dispersion and incoherence of notions of subjectivity. For instance, Flax emphasizes the fact that the regularities of social practices as well as relatively cohesive group affiliations and distinctions are made possible by the fact that "[v]ocabularies and social practices already exist through which [. . .] subjectivity is constituted and by which one makes sense of it to oneself." (97) These simultaneously shared and "individuated" social and discursive practices generate group formations that not only acquire sufficient self-definition to identify themselves from within and to differentiate themselves from without (vis-à-vis other groups), but conversely, which also acquire sufficient flexibility to sustain internal divergences and to form external alliances.

The intricate dialectics between contextually-determined "insides" and "outsides" are often mapped upon another important set of binary oppositions, those between the "private" and the "public" spheres. Habermas's account of the private/public dichotomy relies upon Kant's privileging of autonomous "public" deliberations of educated men and inherits some implicit traces of its presupposed (complementary and hierarchical) gendered separation of spheres. In fact, Habermas's narrative of the unified public sphere posits two actual spheres that theoretically (should?) act as one but tend to conflict. One type of public sphere—the one which we have dealt with so far—could be called the "masculine" public sphere of "private citizens" that has historically excluded all but a select group of men. The other type of public sphere consists of all those (literate) "private citizens" who "as readers, listeners, and spectators could avail themselves via the market of the objects that were subject to discussion." If we assumed that all of the participants in public deliberation were (at least) minimally educated men, we could say that the exclusionary masculine public sphere was a subset of this (relatively) more inclusive public/private sphere of educated, or at least literate, men and women. Thus, although both of these public spheres may fulfill similar (critical) discursive functions, they are clearly constitutively differentiated (in terms of their participants). As Habermas observes,

> The circles of persons who made up the two forms of public were not even completely congruent. Women and dependents were factually and legally excluded from the political public sphere, whereas female readers as well as apprentices and servants often took a more active part in the literary public sphere than the owners of private property and family heads themselves. Yet in the educated classes the one form of public sphere was considered to be identical with the other; in the self-understanding of public opinion the public sphere appeared as one and indivisible. (56)

Since women, dependents, apprentices, and servants were "excluded from the political public sphere," their critical contribution had to take a different form. Rather than actively participating in public deliberations, these members of marginalized groups "often took a more *active part* in the literary public sphere" than their politically empowered counterparts. But their activity, in so far as it was political, was highly mediated by the political activity of the empowered group of men they depended upon. Habermas glosses over this significant lack of class- and gender-based empowerment by sometimes conflating the political activities in first public sphere with the cultural activities in the second public sphere. But this difference had serious political consequences. Other than a few literate female and working-class *writers*, the *reading* public of the "literary public sphere" who were excluded from the "active" (in a Kantian sense) bourgeois public sphere could only consume, perpetuate, or critique the policies and discourses elaborated by numerous privileged bourgeois men and a few privileged women. In so far as these marginalized social groups were not granted a civic, not simply cultural, voice to express alternative or dissenting political interests and opinions, it seems logical that their "form of public sphere was considered to be identical with the other" and that the two spheres "appeared as one and indivisible." Appearances of two-part harmony between spheres can deceptively perpetuate social hierarchies and injustices when one sphere remains silenced while the other keeps talking and acting for and in its stead. It seems that despite their cultural participation in the bourgeois public sphere as readers (and, much less frequently, as writers), women, dependents, servants and apprentices remained (for the most part) relegated to "private" domains whose gender-coded and double-edged associations with "patriarchal authority" (55) and with "humanity-generating closeness," "freedom, love, and cultivation of the person that grew out of the experiences of the conjugal family's private sphere" (48) could mask but not eliminate their comparative lack of both cultural and political power.

This neglect of gender-based domination is an inherent part of the conceptual framework of Habermas's historical narrative. By drawing a hierarchical binary dichotomy between lifeworld and system and relegating domestic relations solely to the privileged "lifeworld"—splitting "public" relations between the system and the lifeworld—Habermas uncritically idealizes the "private" sphere as a haven from the capitalist "system." He repeatedly acknowledges but fails to take into serious consideration the fact that the nuclear family is also governed by the laws of the marketplace. Nancy Fraser persuades us that a more refined analysis of gender relations is crucial to a more accurate understanding of late capitalist societies:

> However morally dubious the consensus and however problematic the content and status of norms, virtually every human action context involves some form of both of them [system and lifeworld]. In the capitalist marketplace, for example, strategic, utility-maximizing exchanges occur against a horizon of intersubjectively shared meanings and norms; agents normally subscribe at least tacitly to some commonly held notions of reciprocity and to some shared conceptions about the social meanings of objects, including what sorts of things are considered exchangeable. Similarly, in the capitalist workplace, managers and subordinates, as well as co-workers, normally coordinate their actions in some extent consentally and with some explicit or implicit reference to normative assumptions, though the consensus be arrived at unfairly and the norms be incapable of withstanding critical scrutiny. Thus, the capitalist economic system has a moral-cultural dimension. Likewise, few if any human action contexts are wholly devoid of strategic calculation. Gift rituals in noncapitalist societies, for example, previously taken as veritable crucibles of solidarity, are now widely understood to have a significant strategic, calculative dimension, one enacted in the medium of power if not in that of money. And, as we shall argue in more detail later, the modern restricted nuclear family is not devoid of individual self-interested, strategic calculations in either medium. These action contexts, then, though not officially counted as economic, have a strategic, economic dimension. (*Unruly Practices*, 118)

By outlining the interpenetration of "system" and "lifeworld" and, correlatively, by showing the "public" dimensions of "private" domains, Fraser illustrates that issues like "What counts as a public matter? What, in contrast, is private?" are serious political questions. The gendered divisions between "public" and "private" spheres are strategically used to map the gendered limits—and the off-limits—of political power. Fraser cautions that "exclud[ing] some issues and interests [such as domestic violence against women] from public debate by personalizing and/or familializing them" results in "enclav[ing] certain matters in specialized discursive arenas and thereby to shield them from broadly based debate and contestation." Such discursive strategies use the public/private dichotomy to gloss over—and thus perpetuate—political and social practices that harm disadvantaged groups. By "deconstructing" the private/public dichotomy, Fraser does not simply persuade us that the aporetic significations of these terms renders them undecidable. More significantly, she illustrates that the effects of these ideological tropes are not simply historically traceable, but also quite decisive in establishing the power relations (and asymmetries) between men and women.

As we have seen in our analyses of "universalist" texts, dominant discursive formations that establish various overlapping social hierarchies—although they may appear inevitable and transcendent—constitute dynamic systems that are sustained by the interrelated constructions of regimes of knowledge and of the group of experts authorized to propose and evaluate them. In the case of Kant and Rousseau, these regimes of power/knowledge operated in part by means of a hierarchical classification of rational agents and cognitive functions. In turn, these agents and functions depended upon the exclusion and subordination of other types of agents, cognitive functions, and actions deemed (respectively) as non-rational, passive or non-universalizable. In critiquing and deconstructing the hierarchical binary oppositions propounded by the contractarian ethics of Kant and Rousseau, we have unveiled the potential instability, self-contradiction and partiality of their proposed truth-claims. Moreover, with the help of Habermas's intersubjective ethics—complemented by and juxtaposed with various feminist critiques of universal reason—we have gone, in some ways, beyond these deconstructive procedures. By means of ethical constructions of subjectivity that neither essentialize nor radically disperse "the self" and its (both affiliative and contestatory) intersubjective relations, we have envisioned open-ended collective dialogues that can pave the way for less hierarchical but non-relativistic democratic discursive practices.

NOTES

1 Zygmunt Bauman, *Postmodern Ethics*. London: Blackwell, 1993, 6.

2 This tenet is repeated many times throughout the *Groundwork of the Metaphysics of Morals*, trans. H. J. Paton. New York: Harper Torchbooks, 1948.

3 *The Social Contract and Discourses*, trans. G. D. H. Cole. London: Everyman, 1973, 191.

4 Jean-Joseph Goux provides a detailed Marxian analysis of the logic of the general

equivalent in *Symbolic Economies*, trans. Jennifer Gage, Ithaca: Cornell University Press, 1988.

5 Jürgen Habermas, *Moral Consciousness and Communicative Action*. Cambridge: The MIT Press, 1991, 67.

6 Nancy Fraser, *Unruly Practices: Power, Discourse and Gender in Contemporary Social Theory*. Minneapolis: University of Minnesota Press, 1989.

7 This article can be found in the anthology *Feminism and Science*, edited by Nancy Tuana, 1989, 61.

8 Jane Flax, *Disputed Subjects: Essays on psychoanalysis, politics and philosophy*. New York: Routledge, 1993.

9 This essay is included in the previously cited work, *Unruly Practices*.

10 Clearly Habermas, in his emphasis upon intersubjective communication and critical debate, does not devalue the former and uphold the latter, but rather intertwines the positive aspects of the two "spheres" through the concept of the lifeworld.

11 Translated by John T. Goldthwait. Berkeley: University of California Press, 1960.

12 See Rooney, Ellen, *Seductive Reasoning*. Ithaca: Cornell University Press, 1989.

13 From Eve Sedgwick's essay "Adam Bede and Henry Esmond: Homosocial Desire and the Historicity of the Female," p. 298. Cited from the anthology *The New Historicism Reader*, edited by H. Avram Veeser, New York: Routledge, 1994.

14 According to Kant, transcendental apperception excludes psychobiographical information and focuses instead upon the *a priori* unity of consciousness that supposedly guarantees objective knowledge.

15 As Anthony Giddens encapsulates it in *Capitalism and Modern Social Theory*, "According to Marx, classes emerge where the relations of production involve a differentiated division of labor which allows for the accumulation of surplus production that can be appropriated by a minority grouping, which thus stands in an exploitative relationship to the mass of producers" (London: Cambridge University Press, 1971).

chapter four

THE FIELD OF CULTURAL PRODUCTION

A SECOND GLANCE AT THE EROTIC, THE AESTHETIC, AND THE SOCIAL

I n a recent issue of *Contemporary French Civilization* (Summer/Fall 1992), Allen S. Weiss argues, "Art must be erotic and contentious, or it shall no longer be. Written in the current political climate—where the fear, censorship and repression of eroticism are once again prime factors in cultural politics—it is hoped that this brief essay may offer some avenues for analysis and polemic." (281) In this statement, Weiss encapsulates some key tenets of contemporary modernist art criticism and scholarship: a strict correlation between the erotic and the aesthetic; a puzzling association between the erotic and the subversive; and the radical disassociation of the aesthetic from ideology, to the extent that an implicit censorship, though much decried when restricting "artistic freedom," is instituted against ideological art and criticism. As Marxian and feminist critics have been arguing since the 1970's, these tenets and practices, institutionally entrenched though they may be, are not beyond question.

There are many questions that can be raised about Weiss's brief but telling statement. First, why must "art be erotic and contentious"? In what ways and for what purposes does the erotic become automatically equated with subversion or, to use Weiss's term, with "contentiousness"? Is it only in its aestheticized form that the erotic can be subversive? More generally, what are the relations between the erotic and the aesthetic? A second set of inquiries can be raised to question the assumption that the aesthetic is not simply apolitical, but also beyond politicized analysis. In what ways is art entirely removed from ideological relations? It seems to me that the burden of proof should lie with the modernist and (in some cases) postmodernist scholars who make such a claim. Even accepting the premise that the aesthetic is entirely or largely removed from ideological influences, does it necessarily follow that art can never be employed or analyzed, in multiple and mediated fashions, to serve explicitly ideological purposes? Why not? Furthermore, if we follow Weiss's assumption that the erotic is subversive or transgressive, then how can we disassociate the erotic from cultural and political norms without taking away the cultural frames of reference that would enable us to interpret it as transgressive? Is a strictly formalistic definition of aesthetic production, and more specifically of aesthetic transgression, plausible? In the rest of this essay, I would like to develop these lines of interrogation of the central assumptions of modernist and (in so far as they follow similar postulates) postmodernist aesthetic practices by relying upon Griselda Pollock's feminist and Pierre Bourdieu's Marxian analyses of the gender and class power relations which help construct the so-called purely "aesthetic" field of cultural production.

In *Vision and Difference*,[1] Griselda Pollock argues against the major tenets of neo-Kantian modernist aesthetics, which posit "the specificity of aesthetic experience; the self-sufficiency of the visual; [and] the teleological evolution of art autonomous from any other social causation or pressure." (14–15) She employs feminist post-structuralist and Marxian methodologies to reveal that art can be understood solely as a symbolic production within specific socio-economic and cultural relations. Furthermore, she argues that "art history itself is to be understood as a series of representational practices which actively produce definitions of sexual difference and contribute to the present configuration of sexual politics and power relations. Art history is not just indifferent to women; it is a masculinist discourse, party to the social construction of sexual difference." (11) Using psychoanalytic theories,[2] she illustrates that modernist discourse (in particular) and various forms of "high culture" (in general) have played an important symbolic role in the perpetuation of women's oppression. Like other symbolic practices, they have reinforced sexist stereotypes by representing men as desiring and creative subjects and women as the beautiful, sometimes sadistically manipulated, images of the desiring male gaze. (17) In response to modernist aesthetics, she calls for a concerted effort on the part of feminist, Marxian, and poststructuralist scholars to engage in a "sustained and far reaching political critique of contemporary representational systems which have an overdetermined effect in the social production of sexual difference and its related gender hierarchy." (14–15)

I believe that, even though not strictly speaking a feminist scholar, Pierre Bourdieu has also been at the forefront of the critique of neo-Kantian aesthetics and that feminist scholars could find valuable means of subverting—and rich alternatives to—modernist practice in his works. In order to stage a confrontation between his Marxian sociological studies of aesthetic production and neo-Kantian aesthetics, I will focus upon four problems and problematics identified by Pollock in forms of Marxian scholarship that merely reverse, without displacing or even plausibly replacing, the neo-Kantian precepts. In my reading, I locate both Bourdieu's and Pollock's criticism somewhere at the optimal mean between the two extremes of neo-Kantian modernist and (some) postmodernist aesthetics, on the one hand, and reductive ideological critiques of art, on the other.

The problematics we will examine are: (1) reflection theory versus genius aesthetics, or treating art as a reflection of the society that produced it, or as an image of its class divisions, as opposed to viewing art as a product of extraordinary innate artistic talent or "genius"; (2) representational theory versus the subjective universal, or treating the artist as a representative of his class vs. positing art as a disinterested subjective response; (3) economic reductionism versus immateriality, or reducing all arguments about the forms and functions of cultural objects to economic or material causes versus manifesting a total disregard for the economic factors that affect the production, circulation, and consumption of art objects; (4) ideological generalization versus exemplary aesthetics, or drawing unmediated connections between vast historical movements and a given piece of art versus positing that a given theory of taste must be shared by all who have genuine taste, whether or not all can or do share it. (*Vision and Difference*, 27)

These problematics are not meant to present "straw-man" alternatives that will make Bourdieu's approach look much more promising by comparison. Nor do they offer a comprehensive survey of critical approaches to art history. Instead, they problematize and nuance the commonly found neo-Kantian and sociological poles of art criticism through the use of Bourdieu's innovative interpretations of culture. Admittedly, the rhetorical strategy of staking a middle position between two alternatives that are presented as highly problematic lends itself to disadvantageous readings of the "extreme" alternatives and advantageous readings of the "middle ground." This positioning, however, is not meant to establish or idealize in an Aristotelian fashion the universalist principle of the "golden mean," but rather, as I have already indicated, to provide critiques and alternatives to modernist aesthetics.

PROBLEMATIC 1: REFLECTION THEORY: THE MIRROR OR THE MAGNET?

If we were to conveniently frame the problem of representation in terms of Platonic philosophy, we would recall that Plato offers not one, but two rival mimetic theories: 1) the mirror model, in which art is only a poor imitation of "things" that themselves constitute only imperfect imitations of transcendental forms, and 2) the magnet theory of expression, in which the artist-genius becomes possessed by a divine or semi-divine presence and transmits to his audience inspirational poetic "truths." As Derrida points out in "The Double Session,"[3] these two models compete with and even contradict one another. On the one hand, the mirror theory takes imitation to be axiomatically mediated and, with each level of mediation, increasingly distorted. On the other hand, the magnet theory presents imitation as immediate and undistorted. In both cases, however, art imitates or represents the transcendental Forms. Kant adopts and reformulates Plato's magnet model by defining the artist as a "genius who has the innate "talent" which gives the rule to art. Since talent [which] is an innate productive faculty of the artist, belongs itself to nature, we may put it this way: Genius is the innate mental aptitude through which nature gives the rule to art."[4]

Kant specifies three criteria that distinguish artistic genius. First, since artistic talent must be innate rather than acquired through education, "originality must be its primary property." (225) But originality, in the sense of producing an artifact without imitating other artifacts and without learning how to produce art does not suffice to qualify an artist as a genius. As Kant phrases it, an artist may also create "original nonsense" or non-art. Taking this possibility into consideration, Kant argues that art objects must be exemplary and "consequently, though not themselves . . . derived from imitation, they must serve that purpose for others, i.e. as a standard or rule of estimating." (225) However, the artist himself, being motivated by genius and inspiration rather than by an acquired taste and method, cannot actually teach his artistic skills. Thus, although exemplary—a thing that motivates others to imitate it—a genuine artistic object is also inimitable. (225) All of these postulates establish a clear distinction between art and social life by naturalizing and mystifying both the artist (the innate genius, the inimitable seer) and his artistic creation (the unreproducible object that reflects and orders "nature" in an undistorted, sublime fashion).

Kant's philosophical formulation of original artistic genius is itself not original. The conception emerged during the Renaissance and became increasingly prevalent in modern times. As Janet Wolff has documented, before the Renaissance, artwork was collectively performed by and attributed to artisans, craftsmen, painters, builders and their students. Not coincidentally, the paradigm of the individual artist as a genius developed along with the growth of capitalism. Whereas before capitalism artists depended upon patrons who commissioned art, during capitalism the artist became dependent upon such a vast and often invisible network of forces and institutions—the market, critics, museums, and the academy—that he or she appeared to be (without actually being) an independent creator of art.[5]

At the opposite end of the spectrum from neo-Kantian mimetic theories, some scholars have insisted that art mirrors (or reflects) society rather than magnetically projecting images of nature filtered by exceptional human judgment. As Pollock illustrates, reflection theory posits that a given art object produced in a specific setting "represents social processes which are themselves enormously complicated, mobile, and opaque." (*Vision and Difference*, 28) The problem with this type of sociological analysis is that it reductively assumes a clear and direct link between given artifacts and broad social movements, thus bypassing both the particularity of a given piece of art and the complexity of social or intellectual currents. In his overtly anti-Kantian "social critique of the judgment of taste,"[6] Bourdieu provides us with some plausible conceptual means of envisioning art as a social(ized) field without having to resort to sweeping generalizations concerning vast social movements. Countering the Kantian and modernist "ideology of charisma," which "regards taste in legitimate culture as a gift of nature," he argues that "scientific observation shows that cultural needs are the product of upbringing and education" by citing and analyzing sociological surveys which establish that cultural practices and tastes ranging from what is considered "high art" to "pop culture" are directly related to educational and socioeconomic background." (1)

Based upon this research, he concludes that "artistic vision," far from being an innate and mystifying talent, is produced by and within specific social institutions and practices. Furthermore, by demonstrating that "the 'pure gaze' is a historical invention linked to the emergence of an autonomous field of artistic production, that is, a field capable of imposing its own norms on both the production and the consumption of its products," Bourdieu reveals that instead of being ahistorical and universally valid, the modernist version of the Kantian "pure-gaze" theory produces a historically specific narrative that empowers (mostly) the authority of a few men to judge or create "true art." (3) The fact that their claims to universal truth and their hierarchical classifications are widely accepted only attests to the fact that their narrative strategies and institutionalized social practices are effective in producing the desired ideological effects rather than "proving" the validity of their claims. As previously suggested, by noting the correlation between a historically specific mode of artistic evaluation—modernism, for example—and the social effects of this practice, Bourdieu does not establish a direct and unmediated connection between them. On the contrary, his nuanced study of taste illustrates how despite certain regularities in the correspondences between "high education" and preference for "high art," or little education and preference for non-consecrated "pop art," statistics register numerous exceptions and subversions of these general trends. In other words, in reading Bourdieu, we cannot draw unqualified generalizations concerning the links between ideological paradigms and social practices.

To offer a pertinent example presented by Pollock in conducting feminist analyses of art, we cannot unproblematically assume that women adopt and accept the demeaning representations of femininity disseminated by both "high" and "low" art. She states,

> Women may and often do experience themselves through the images of women and ideas about women which are presented to us by the society in which we live. Woman in patriarchal culture is [generally] represented as the negative of man, the non-male, the mutilated other. But that does not make women castrated; nor does it ensure that women see themselves only in those terms. Women have struggled against the given definitions of femininity, negotiating their various situations at different periods and in different cultures. They have resisted what is represented to them." (*Vision and Difference*, 40)

However, this is not to say that women are not affected by demeaning or devalorized representations of femininity. On the contrary, women and other variously devalorized groups internalize in part the norms and discourses that demean them and strive to "prove" themselves as "equal" to the cultural elite by adopting their standards and rules. According to Bourdieu's apt formulation, "Competitive struggle is the form of class struggle which the dominated classes allow to be imposed on them when they accept the stakes offered by the dominant classes. It is an integrative struggle and, by virtue of the initial handicaps, a reproductive struggle, since those who enter this chase, in which they are beaten before they start, as the constancy of the gaps testifies, implicitly recognize the legitimacy of the goals pursued by those whom they pursue, by the mere fact of taking part." (*Distinction*, 165) Nonetheless, by engaging in competition and partly internalizing "the rules of the game" that serve the interests of the dominant classes, the non-dominant classes inevitably modify, re-interpret, and even question or re-evaluate those rules. In other words, the process of internalization of dominant norms and practices is neither faithful nor complete. In turn, dominant norms and representations themselves may be internally diverse and contradictory enough to destabilize and challenge themselves from "within." Hence, we cannot adopt the mimetic model of unmediated reflection in either of its two forms: magnetic projection of nature attained through inspiration *or* reflection of elite social norms, movements, or practices. Both versions are interrogated and modified by aesthetic theories which present art and artistic taste as shaped by specific educational practices which vary among different groups and different individuals.

PROBLEMATIC 2: THE SUBJECTIVE UNIVERSAL US. REPRESENTATIONAL AESTHETICS

Kant argues that since the judgment of taste, which he locates between sensory perception and cognitive skills (or reason), "is not a cognitive judgment, and so is not logical, but is aesthetic—which means that it is one whose determining ground cannot be other than subjective. Every reference of representations is capable of being objective, even of sensations. . . . The one exception to this is the feeling of pleasure or displeasure. This denotes nothing in the object, but is a feeling which the Subject has of itself and of the manner in which it is affected by representation." (*Critique of Judgment*, 160) In other words, unlike sensory perception, judgment of taste has virtually nothing to do with the (empirical) qualities of the object which, Kant assumes, all viewers can observe and agree upon. On the other hand, unlike "objective" logical statements, which call for collective validation as either true or false, taste is subjective. It is experienced by each person in an immediate (or pure) and intimate fashion and does not require collective validation.

However, according to Kant, just because taste is subjective, it does not follow that taste is not also universal. Kant reasons that if we accept his axiom that taste constitutes a disinterested aesthetic pleasure, then "it is inevitable that [we] should look on the object as one containing delight for all men. For since the delight is not based on any inclination of the Subject (or on any deliberate interest), but the subject feels himself completely free in respect of the liking which he accords to the object, he can find as reason for his delight no personal conditions to which his own subjective self might alone be party. Hence he must regard it as resting on what he may also presuppose in every other person; and therefore he must believe that he has reason for demanding a similar delight from everyone." (168) Furthermore, if we also accept his claim that judgment is located between perception and understanding, then we must also accept the claim that this "universality cannot spring from concepts." According to Kantian philosophy, concepts cannot evoke feelings of pleasure or displeasure but only ways of logically organizing and validating knowledge. Thus Kant concludes that "[t]he result is that the judgment of taste [. . .] must involve a claim to [. . .] subjective universality." (168)

Obviously Kant makes numerous assumptions in this chain of argumentation that could be questioned and rejected. For instance, even if we accept his definition of judgment as a mediating category between perception and cognition, that is, as intimately, subjectively, and disinterestedly experienced, we do not have to conclude, with him, that all people's reactions must (universally) agree with respect to their judgments of taste. The fact that judgment is posited as disinterested does not imply that all judgments of given art objects have to coincide. On the contrary, we could even more plausibly argue that because judgment is a personal experience of the pleasure or displeasure (and everything in between) stimulated by works of art, people can have different assessments or modes of responding to those objects.[7]

If we take into consideration not only the systematicity, force, or regularity of ideological representations and of their social effects, but also the multiple contingencies, social, economic, "personal," involved in the production, evaluation, and reception of art, then we can avoid both Kantian universalizations and sociological generalizations. Whereas universalization presents the artist as a neutral and disinterested genius, generalization "place[s] the artist as a representative of a class outlook. . . ." In offering an example of sociological generalization, Pollock discusses the lamentable practice (in much masculinist modernist criticism) of devaluing the production of most women artists by describing them as "minor" or "secondary" figures,[8] while upholding the merits of a few token female artists as representative of "the visual ideology of a whole sex." (29) This tokenizing gesture not only denies the historical and "personal" positionality of any given female artist, but also reduces and homogenizes the so-called "outlook" of a vast and highly differentiated group of people. In brief, representative aesthetics is not a viable alternative to the Kantian subjective universal. Gestures of condescension toward the groups marginalized by the practices of a given social field can only uphold the overdetermined gender, race, or class hierarchies that excluded them from it to begin with. By not only disregarding the specific productions of given (female) artists, but also neglecting numerous other artists from the same "class(ification)" on the basis of knowing their "point of view" by virtue of being familiar with the work of a few "representative" members, modernist critics enact and perpetuate the exclusion of women from the field of cultural production.

Bourdieu obliquely proposes a possible alternative to the Kantian universalization of subjective taste vs. the representative politics of much scholarship by insisting that we stop privileging "aesthetic" experiences and delineating strict hierarchies among them—hierarchies which, by no coincidence, often end up marginalizing the groups who have less "cultural capital" or are less valorized by social and cultural elites:

> The science of taste and of cultural consumption begins with a transgression that is in no way aesthetic: it has to abolish the sacred frontier which makes legitimate culture a separate universe, in order to discover the intelligible relations which unite apparently incommensurable 'choices,' such as preferences in music and food, painting and sport, literature and hairstyle. [. . .] The denial of lower, coarse, vulgar, venal, servile—in a word, natural—enjoyment, which constitutes the sacred sphere of culture, implies an affirmation of the superiority of those who can be satisfied with the sublimated, refined, disinterested, gratuitous, distinguished pleasures forever closed to the profane. That is why art and cultural consumption are predisposed, consciously and deliberately or not, to fulfil a social function of legitimating social differences. (*Distinction*, 6–7)

By subverting or blurring the strict hierarchies that code artistic productions, we can also come closer to subverting some of their more resonant (binary) connotations, like the association of women or the lower classes with the (debased, less civilized) body and of men from the upper classes with refinement, higher creative and mental aptitudes—in a word, with "class" and "taste." Working to expose and minimize the hierarchies that comprise the field of cultural production entails a very different gesture from both the entrenched modernist fetishization and aesthetization of art which validates such hierarchies and from those postmodernist claims that declare art and the field of artistic production as intrinsically fragmentary, minoritary, subversive, writerly, thought-provoking or possessing any other desirable feature without reference to the historical and institutional contexts of specific movements or works. Once again, this essay opts for a middle ground between the (post)modernist and sociological extremes of cultural analysis. Against radically sociological readings and partly along with (post)modernist readings, it argues that that art certainly does have its specificity. However, instead of locating this specificity in a set of formal characteristics, be they proposed as typologies of genre or as essentially transgressive tropes, this essay locates it at the juncture of both determined and contingent institutional practices, social relations, and individuated circumstances. As Tony Bennett aptly argues with respect to the homologous field of literary production, "if it is important to insist, in this sense, on the specificity of literature, this is because, thus understood, it is by no means a mere illusion. [. . .] To conclude, because literature cannot be secured as a formal reality, that its analysis should be dissipated into an undifferentiated study of signifying practices is to miss what ought properly to have been the focus of analysis in the first place: the functioning of a definitely organized field of uses and effects in which strategies of boundary construction and maintanance are central to the functioning of a socially differentiated region of textual uses and effects (rather than kind of writing)." (*Outside Literature*, 142)

PROBLEMATIC 3: IMMATERIALITY VS. ECONOMIC REDUCTIONISM

As we have already seen, for Kant the economic factors that partly determine artistic production, consumption, and the careers of individual artists are unimportant or immaterial. Economic forces are not at all Kant's concern. The opposite analytical move entails relying upon a simplistic version of the Marxian base/superstructure model to consider all art as completely determined by economic forces and relations. As Pollock notes, here "[t]he danger is always of simply shifting your analysis from one set of causes to another, i.e. art is the way it is because of economic arrangements. Art is inevitably shaped and limited by the kind of society which produces it; but its particular features are not caused by economic structures or organization." (*Vision and Difference*, 29) Bourdieu's conceptualization of "economy" helps us avoid reductive versions of materialist criticism. Rather than adopting a narrow definition of economy, Bourdieu uses "economy" as a homology to interpret the logic of multiple and diverse social fields and relations organized around hierarchies that endow (or invest) specific groups, objects, institutions or activities with more value, or cultural and symbolic capital, than others.[9]

In the field of cultural production (also the title of one of Bourdieu's works), "symbolic capital" denotes the prestige, honor, or consecration that a given artifact, person, or activity gains within a specific domain. Correlatively, cultural capital indicates the degree-specific consecration—or competences, "knowledge," and "dispositions" (cultural tendencies)—manifested by a given individual or group of people. Cultural capital is profoundly affected and partially determined by an

The Field of Cultural Production

individual's familial and educational background and class position. All of these symbolic "assets" include but are not limited to economic factors in the narrow sense of the term. This wider conceptualization of cultural value enables us to understand much better, for example, feminist calls for "a room of one's own." It becomes very clear that Virginia Woolf, along with so many other feminist critics, was not simply demanding that women be given the material means and comfort to produce art. This is not to say that material comfort and privacy, so often denied to female artists in societies where mothering and nurturing are women's primary functions, are not only helpful, but also essential to women's artistic productions. However, feminists also ask that women's artistic productions also be granted symbolic value (or capital) rather than being systematically devalorized and excluded by masculinist elitist institutions (like scholarly critiques or university curricula) and their cultural registers (like the canon, the major museums or art exhibits). Without offering female artists both the material means and the cultural encouragement (or valorization) to pursue their work—two necessities that are inextricably interrelated—our society cannot even begin to attain gender-based parity in the field of cultural production.

PROBLEMATIC 4: EXEMPLARY AESTHETICS VS. IDEOLOGICAL GENERALIZATION

When he discusses the universality of (implicitly good) taste, Kant draws a hierarchical distinction between that which is merely agreeable and that which is beautiful. Whereas the agreeable expresses one's personal and contingent preference— "Everyone has his own taste"—"the beautiful stands on quite a different footing." (*Critique of Judgment*, 195) The difference cannot be registered by collective agreement, since general approval is not the same thing as universal validity. Kant carefully points out that the universality of taste does not imply that given judgments are generally shared. Distinguishing between the general, or (empirically established) collective agreement about what is agreeable, and the universal, or what should be (but may not be) recognized by all as beautiful, Kant lays the normative foundations of aesthetic taste: "The assertion is not that everyone will fall in with our judgment, but rather that everyone ought to agree with it. Here I put forward my judgment of taste as an example of the judgment of common sense, and attribute to it on that account exemplary validity. Hence common sense is a mere ideal norm." (195)

As the above statement makes very clear, Kant is not at all concerned with leaving the beautiful to collective discussion or debate. Instead, he wishes to validate and reinforce elitist practices and institutions that delineate strict hierarchies between objects of art. We can all voice our opinions concerning what is agreeable to us— since the agreeable is not valorized (by Kantian aesthetics) to begin with—but in making claims concerning the beautiful, our subjective impressions will be measured by and against Kant's universal standards. The discrepancy between our subjective evaluations and his universal claims can only display the errors in our judgment (our lack of good taste) rather than expose the subjectivity of his (elitist, historically specific) universalism.

According to Pollock, the opposite response to this postulation of abstract universal validity claims involves treating a work of art as fully ideologically motivated, that is, as representative of specific "class" (in the broad sense of the term) interests and points of view. To illustrate this procedure, Pollock gives the example of critics who "treat work by women merely as exemplars of womanness" and who "reproduce a tautology which teaches us nothing about what being, doing like, thinking as a woman might be." (29–30) This type of criticism not only draws a direct and unmediated correlation between a given representation and all the members of a class of people, but also assumes that the given class shares some common essential features that are necessarily represented in the works of art produced by their members. Surprisingly, we find this problematic assumption not only in modernist or masculinist aesthetics, but also in some postmodernist and feminist aesthetics. As Rita Felski observes,

> It reappears in the feminist position which hypostasizes the "feminine," subversive quality of the polysemic text that undermines the linguistic conventions of a phallocentric symbolic order. . . . [T]he text acquires an exemplary importance as a locus of indeterminacy which undermines fixed meanings and authoritarian ideological positions, which . . . are attributed to an entire Western cultural and philosophical tradition rooted in patriarchal interests, a tradition that has sought to control meaning and repress differences. *L'écriture féminine* and Kristeva's theory of the semiotic constitute two models of a "revolutionary" writing practice which have received extensive converage in recent feminist literary theory. Both stress the radical implications of a rupture and fragmentation of symbolic discourse, which is defined as repressive and fundamentally phallocentric though reference to the writings of Derrida and Lacan. . . . [This option] does not adequately solve the problem of the relationship between literature and feminist politics. It is impossible to make a convincing case for the claim that there is anything inherently feminine or feminist in experimental writing as such.[10]

It is worth pointing out that in strains of postmodernist scholarship, unlike in modernist ones, feminine ideology becomes disassociated from the referent women. It is (not surprisingly) modernist writing itself which has a set of characteristics or powers, regardless of whether it was written by women or men. On the one hand, this is a fortunate move because it no longer functions to essentialize women (or men) as a homogeneous group that engages only in a certain kind of writing. On the other hand, it is also an unfortunate move because it hypostasizes a kind of writing as, for example, subversive or marginal long after it has become culturally accepted and even dominant. More seriously, it also avoids looking at the asymmetrical status of men and women in relation to one another in the field of cultural production.

To offer just one poignant example, literature is often described as a feminine field. Yet if one examines numbers of male and female writers, even without any reference to the cultural consecration of their respective works, one finds that 75 percent of writers are male and 25 percent are female. If we take consecration into consideration, the discrepancy between the number of male and female writers becomes dismal. In France, for example, only three or four female writers became canonized or made it to high-school curicula. A valorization of *écriture féminine*, if it bears no connection to the writing and valorization of women, does little to overcome this discrepancy of institutional power and value between the sexes. At every stage of the formation and consecration of the canon, women's writing gets eliminated with or without explicit discriminatory justifications. This serves not only to devalue women's artistic productions, but also, as Marcelle Marini points out, to provide students and the reading public with unisexual cultural identifications and, correlatively, to culturally marginalize women. "Today, the crux of the issue is: will we be able to create a culture in which identifications are possible across sex boundaries, a culture that involves an interplay between non-differentiation and differentiation, a culture of sharing, a culture that is truly a home for both sexes?"[11] In raising this important but often ignored question, Marini assumes neither that women's writing inherently differs from men's, nor that feminine writing, though produced by both women and men, has some intrinsic and ahistorical properties that mark it as subversive. Instead of prejudging and typologizing women's writing in advance, she reasonably asks that it be offered the same institutional chance to be written, read, and appreciated as men's writing. By disassociating feminine writing from the writing of women, postmodernist scholarship, much like modernist criticism, avoids confronting the discrepancies in power and value between the cultural production of men and women. Such institutionalized impediments and hierarchies become rationalized or accepted to such a degree that they are regarded as normal.

Bourdieu describes and contests the processes that normalize symbolic hierarchies. For example, in his discussion of the *habitus*, delineated in *Outline of a Theory of Practice*, Bourdieu enables us to see art as informed by particular ideologies (hence far from "universal") without completely reducing art to a set of identifiable ideological interests. The *habitus*, or the "system of dispositions" (tendencies acquired through various cultural practices, including education, family upbringing, etc.), consists of the cultural presuppositions shared so unquestioningly by members of a given social class or group that they appear as "history turned into nature" but "denied as such." (79) These habitual practices and representations form our points of view in the world. Because they are collective "structuring structures" rather than purely idiosyncratic beliefs, they generate similar (but not identical) standards, norms, modes of representation and practices for the specific group(s) of people who share them.

Nevertheless, a given *habitus* is not necessarily internally homogeneous or completely differentiated from others. For example, although the *habitus* of modernist scholars may be influenced by their common ideological and class positions like their commitment to validating and reproducing the so-called "high art" of white male artists the diversity of ideological positions within and outside of a given class or field leaves room for alternative representations and disidentificatory practices that challenge regimes of knowledge, power, and cultural validation. As Griselda Pollock notes, despite the overwhelming prevalence of what psychoanalytic critics call "phallic" regimes of representing women as the sex objects of the desiring male gaze, there is much hope for feminist intervention in the field of artistic production. For example, she illustrates how feminist philosophers (most notably Luce Irigaray) have re-conceptualized sensory perception in a manner that does not privilege sight over the other senses. Similarly some artists like Morisot and Cassatt have engendered alternative representations of "femininity" to the masculinist ones by featuring women as gazing subjects and by rearticulating "traditional space so that it ceases to function primarily as the space of sight for a mastering gaze, but becomes the locus of relationships." (*Vision and Difference*, 87) Last but not least, she notes that spectators have engaged in disidentificatory practices by refusing to identify with the (hetero)sexist, racist, or classist representations validated as high art. (158) Hence, by locating art within a field of highly complex and overdetermined social relations rather than elevating it to a transcendental, marginalized, or representative space, artists, critics and viewers alike can critically examine and improve symbolic practices without abandoning their prerogative to evaluate and enjoy works of art.

NOTES

1   *Vision and Difference: Femininity, Feminism and the Histories of Art.* London: Routledge, 1988.

2   She relies upon the post-Lacanian scholarship of Laura Mulvey, Luce Irigaray, and Mary Anne Doane.

3   This essay is found in *Dissemination*, Jacques Derrida, translated with an introduction by Barbara Johnson. Chicago: University of Chicago Press, 1981.

4   *Critique of Judgment, Philosophical Writings*, Immanuel Kant, edited by Ernst Behler, forward by René Wellek. New York: Continuum, The German Library, 1986, 224.

5   Janet Wolff, *The Social Production of Art.* New York: New York University Press, 1981.

6   Pierre Bourdieu, *Distinction: A Social Critique of the Judgment of Taste*, trans. by Richard Nice. Cambridge: Harvard University Press, 1984.

7   Of course, this conception of artistic creation assumes the category of difference as fundamental, whereas Kant's universalist discourse assumes the category of sameness as fundamental.

8   For example, by describing female artists as the muses or disciples of male artists rather than creators in their own right or, more generally, by declaring them as *a priori* inferior to male artists.

9   Bourdieu elaborates this conceptual framework in several of his works, including *Outline of a Theory of Practice*, trans. Richard Nice (Cambridge: Cambridge University Press, 1977), *The Logic of Practice*, trans. Richard Nice (Stanford: Stanford University Press, 1990), and *The Field of Cultural Production*, edited and introduced by Randal Johnson (New York: Columbia University Press, 1993).

10   *Beyond Feminist Aesthetics: Feminist Literature and Social Change.* Cambridge: Harvard University Press, 1989, 4–6.

11   *Ibid.*, 323.

JUSTICE, EQUALITY AND
PROPORTIONAL GROUP REPRESENTATION

chapter five

THE (IM)POSSIBLE FUTURE OF DEMOCRACY?

It is important, then, in order to have a clear declaration of the general will, that there should be no partial association in the State, and that every citizen should express only his opinion.[1]

Let women share the rights [of man] and she will emulate the virtues of man, for she must grow more perfect when emancipated, or justify the authority that chains such a weak being to her duty.[2]

The mothers, daughters, and sisters, women representing the Nation, ask to be constituted as a National Assembly. Whereas ignorance, oblivion and contempt of the rights of women are the sole causes of public misfortune and of the corruption of governments, they have resolved to lay out in a solemn declaration, the natural, sacred and inalienable rights of woman. . . .[3]

We shall demonstrate not only that this principle of identity of interests, once made the basis of political rights, is a violation of the rights of those who are thereby debarred from them, but also that this identity ceases to exist once it gives rise to genuine inequality. We shall insist on this point because the fallacy involved in accepting this principle is the only one still likely to be dangerous, since it is the only one to which intelligent men are not yet wholly alive. [4]

Since the French Revolution, the problem of how to conceive of political community in a democratic fashion has shaped the history of Western nations. Some theorists and politicians assume that this problem is resolved by the institution of universal suffrage. Others argue that the right to vote provides only a minimal, and insufficient, means of exercising political influence in a democratic fashion. Both those political theorists who support current versions of democracy and those who propose more egalitarian ones tend to rely upon a definition of democracy similar to the one proposed by David Beetham: "Democracy I take to be a mode of decision-making about collectively binding rules and policies over which the people exercise control, and the most democratic argument to be that where all members of the collectivity enjoy effective equal rights to take part in such decision-making directly—one, that is to say, which realizes to the greatest conceivable degree the principles of popular control and equality in its exercise."[5]

This definition remains open to different interpretations. As mentioned, on the one hand, the theorists and politicians who wish to maintain the status quo argue that the fact that all citizens have a right to vote qualifies as "equal rights to take part in decision-making directly." On the other hand, groups of feminists, Marxian and civil-rights activists and theorists argue that, in practice, democratic nations are shaped by the interests of generally privileged groups of middle class white men who hold the functions of socio-political and cultural power. Consequently, they suggest that the structures and institutions of democratic nations do not give all political groups an equal chance to participate in political decisions in any meaningful fashion because they continue to systematically privilege empowered groups of men and to discriminate against disadvantaged groups of women, minorities, or working-class people.

Such critiques raise the following questions: What are the socio-political theories, codes and institutions that contribute to the systematic reproduction of the power of a small class of men in democratic societies? If women and minorities tend to vote for members of privileged groups of men—and this remains an open "empirical" question whose responses vary depending upon particular political contexts and moments—then in what ways and on what bases can egalitarian political theorists and activists critique the hierarchical socio-political structures and institutions of democratic societies? What are some of the political alternatives suggested by these critics, or, more precisely, how can we conceptualize and validate the institution of democratic citizenship in a way that would enable diverse groups of people to share socio-political power in a more proportional and egalitarian fashion?

This essay will attempt to address most of these questions by examining the cultural logic behind different conceptions of democratic citizenship and of political representation that began to be both outlined and contested during the French Enlightenment. The passages cited above will help introduce some of the current difficulties and debates concerning the political representation of disempowered groups, particularly of women, in democratic societies. Along with other feminist theorists, I argue that the liberal and individualist model of democracy—as proposed by Rousseau and Wollstonecraft in this essay and significantly reformulated by current democratic theories and institutions—is conceptually and practically unable to represent diverse, and especially currently disadvantaged, communities in a "just" and "egalitarian" fashion.

Roughly speaking, by a "just" democratic system I mean one that allows all citizens to vote freely (i.e. without coercion or manipulation) and does not systematically endow some groups of people with more political, social, and cultural power and consecration than others. For example, it is not just that men disproportionately occupy positions of power by being executives, doctors, lawyers, professors, and artists while women disproportionately occupy positions that are devalued and underpaid by being secretaries, nurses, and teachers. The asymmetry between masculinized and feminized professions occurs both because the professions dominated by men are consecrated and paid more than those generally occupied by women and because women are discouraged and impeded from occupying positions of power in politics, culture and society. By an "egalitarian" democratic system I mean one in which all social groups have proportional representation, meaning political representation that corresponds to their proportion of the population, in government and (preferably) also in other consecrated social fields, including academia, law or medicine.

Although these formulations of political justice and equality are inseparably intertwined, they do not refer to exactly the same thing. A system can be egalitarian—in the sense of not discriminating against any group of people—without necessarily resulting in the "just" proportional representation of different groups. In fact, chance, non-discriminatory political affiliations and social and political trends are more likely to yield an uneven distribution of power among social groups rather than a proportional one. For example, the most visible political figures in Democratic and Republican parties in the United States are certainly not discriminated against, yet the representation of Democrats and Republicans with respect to one another in Congress and other government functions is neither necessarily equal nor proportional. Likewise, a system of proportional representation need not necessarily be just. Proportional representation systems may well be based on totalitarian repression or manipulation of votes and hence show little regard for valid norms of democratic justice. I believe that only a system that combines more or less agreed upon—but always negotiable—norms of justice *and* proportional representation can be "democratic" in the fullest and most meaningful sense of the term, meaning, once again, to realize "to the greatest conceivable degree the principles of popular control and equality in its exercise."

I also propose that one of the best means of achieving democratic justice and equality is not by means of heavy-handed state intervention, which risks (at best) creating a conservative backlash or (at worst) turning toward totalitarian, and hence undemocratic measures, but by creating multiple kinds of organizations, efforts, discussions, and debates in the public sphere(s) by both marginalized and dominant groups interested in attaining a more egalitarian democratic society. By arguing against (additional) systematic state regulations and quotas, I am by no means defending anarchy. Rather, I am suggesting that egalitarian group-movements in the public sphere would probably prove both more effective and less dangerous than an increase in state power and control. These "egalitarian" movements or interventions in the public sphere(s) would take a *non-systematic* form, since they would not all be organized by the same group or institution, support the same interests, or propose the same policies. Nonetheless, they would be *systemic* in the sense of pervading all areas of life, including politics, culture and society. In other words, the kind of egalitarian movements I support would function in a similar but *opposite* way to current non-egalitarian and sexist institutions, which discriminate against women and minorities in different fields, manners, codes and institutions, without needing any unifying structure or set of institutions to be highly effective.

The multiple public spheres I am alluding to resemble Habermas's description of the bourgeois public sphere, "the sphere of private people come together as a public" to discuss, critique and debate both private concerns and public issues. However, rather than being single, bourgeois, masculine, and governed by the goal of achieving consensus (as Habermas describes them in *The Structural Transformation of the Public Sphere*), they would be acknowledged as heterogeneous, disunified, fluid and overdetermined in constitution and formation. In brief, I propose that since currently dominant liberal/individualist and universalist models of citizenship and of the public sphere are unwilling and unable to correct systematic political and cultural exclusions and discriminations, then, as Chantal Mouffe explains, the task of revisionary political theorists consists of nothing less than reformulating in a more egalitarian fashion the political unit of democratic societies, meaning the very notion of democratic citizenship:

> The central issue concerns the way we conceptualize the political community, and our belonging to it, i.e. citizenship. [. . .] Politics is about the constitution of the political community. [. . .] A citizen is not . . . , as in liberalism, someone who is the passive recipient of rights and who enjoys the protection of the law. It is rather a common political identity of persons who might be engaged in many different communities and who have differing conceptions of the good, but who accept submission to certain authoritative rules or conduct. Those rules are not instruments for achieving a common purpose—since the idea of a substantive common good has been discarded—but conditions that individuals must observe in choosing purposes of their own. [. . .] Such a view of citizenship is clearly different from both the liberal and the communitarian ones. It is not one identity among others, as it is in liberalism, nor is it the dominant identity that overrides all others, as in civic republicanism. It is an articulating principle that affects the different subject politions of the social agent, while allowing for a plurality of specific allegiances and for the respect of individual liberty."[6]

In order to begin redefining the notion of citizenship, we must first question its current underlying assumptions and exclusionary mechanisms. Two of these interrelated assumptions are its masculinist and universalist formulations, both of which were consolidated during the French Enlightenment. In fact, I would argue that a critique of gender-based and other kinds of political asymmetries in formulations and practices of both liberal and republican-communitarian versions of citizenship may be as pertinent and necessary today as during the French Revolution, when proto-feminists like Condorcet and Mary Wollstonecraft attempted to "androgynously" include women into the masculine-neutral formulations of democratic citizenship proposed in the *Declaration des Droits de l'Homme*. As Geneviève Fraisse's analysis of their works reveals, these two proto-feminist theorists attempted to extend the rights of man to women in complementary ways.[7]

Condorcet argues for a sexually-neutral conception of citizenship. In his formulation, men and women assume almost identical civil rights and responsibilities. He does not discuss whether or not men and women would actually share political power, but his model of citizenship remains open to this possibility. Like many other social theorists of his times, Condorcet acknowledges the fact that women were conditioned differently and appeared to be less prepared for political functions than men. However, he posits that, given a rigorous education, women could overcome their initial disadvantages and would competently exercise political power.

Wollstonecraft, on the other hand, opts for a gendered or ambisexual conception of citizenship based upon a division of labor between men and women in the private sphere and a sharing of civic duties in the public sphere. Her formulation thus both contributes to and subverts the consolidation of the gendered division between public and private spheres that was emerging during the eighteenth century. She agrees with contemporary mores and laws where in the private sphere women and men should assume complementary roles. On the one hand, women must take charge of domestic functions and of the education of children. On the other hand, men must function as the overall guides and bread-winners for the nuclear family. However, she argues that in their public roles, both women and men should act as rational citizen-subjects, in accordance with a (previously) masculine definition of citizenship.

In Wollstonecraft's opinion, which in this respect differs from the opinions of Rousseau and Montesquieu, women's responsibilities in the private sphere should not exclude them from full political rights.[8] Nor should it, even worse, relegate them to the status of legal minors, as these two other political theorists argued or implied. On the contrary, Wollstonecraft claims, domestic responsibilities should actually qualify women for full citizenship status along with and, in fact, in ways similar to men. As we will see, Olympe de Gouges carries Wollstonecraft's feminist challenge to masculinist versions of citizenship even further by arguing not only that women should have the right to the same kind of citizenship status as men, but also that insofar as women are at a social and political disadvantage with respect to men, they should have the right to some special, gender-specific rights to help combat sex discrimination.

When examining how the notion of sexual difference affects our definitions and practices of citizenship, current discussions in democratic theories often continue the same kinds of debates and propose similar kinds of solutions for the elimination of gender-based asymmetries as the ones envisioned by Rousseau, Wollstonecraft, Gouges and Condorcet. For feminists and nonfeminists alike, the debates centering on the asymmetrical power relations between men and women begin from a number of contested premises concerning the nature of and relations between socio-political equality and sexual difference among citzens of democratic nations. To some extent, the divisions among feminists themselves can be attributed to their divergent responses to the two principal kinds of androcentric discourses that have enacted and justified the domination of women.

Assuming a strategy similar to Condorcet's, "egalitarian feminists" react to the fact that the domination of women has often been rationalized in the name of women's complementarity, difference, and implicit inferiority to men. Like Condorcet, they argue that discourses and practices that encode sexual difference always risk reproducing traditional hierarchies between men and women. Consequently, they conclude that in order to eliminate gender-based domination, the binary production of gender itself has to be seriously interrogated and, ideally, eliminated. This group of theorists tends to propose either sexually neutral or androgynous political models of citizenship. By contrast, employing a logic similar to Wollstonecraft's and, as we will see, even closer to Olympe de Gouges's, "identitarian" or "differentialist" feminists point out that androcentric discourses have always claimed gender-neutrality or "universality" in order to mask the exclusion of women from socio-political participation on a par with men. Hence, this group of feminists maintains that women, instead of continuing to efface themselves as sexed subjects, must reclaim and refashion their gendered identities in a manner that can lead to the elimination of their subordination.[9]

As Joan Scott points out in her influential article, "Deconstructing equality-versus-difference: or, the uses of poststructuralist theory for feminism," insofar as both feminist "camps" desire the elimination of gender based-domination, the antinomy between "equality" and "difference" is in part a spurious one.[10] The contrary of equality is inequality, not difference; while the contrary of difference is identity, not equality. Thus, many feminists, including Olympe de Gouges and Luce Irigaray, argue persuasively that equality and difference are fully compatible social constructs. From a historical perspective, women and men have proven to be both similar to and different from one another. Consequently, any formulation of equality has to take into consideration the ways in which men and women's social positions—meaning the positions of two groups divided and allied along class, gender, race, religious and other lines—intersect and diverge. Nevertheless, the binary terms of this debate cannot be entirely deconstructed. They remain relevant as the starting points and the set of normative and political principles that enable different kinds of theories of democratic citizenship, today as much as— if not more so than—during the Enlightenment.

As we can see from this brief preliminary discussion of Enlightenment political paradigms, the debates concerning the nature and processes of political representation, the demographics of group empowerment or relative lack of group power, and the normative assumptions which underlie democratic politics are issues that continue to be relevant today, not only to political theorists, but more generally to

Justice, Equality and Proportional Group Representation

citizens of democratic nations and of nations in the process of becoming democratic. These issues are at stake in policies and practices ranging from affirmative action to the Equal Rights Amendment proposals offered by the National Organization of Women; from the complex and devastating ethnic struggles in the former Yugoslavia to the quest for independence of the countries that made up the former Soviet Union. By stating that democratic theories and institutions play an important role in such discontinuous and international events, I do not mean to suggest that democracy is a homogeneous construct even less a homogeneous institution. Democratic systems are shaped not only by a country's ethnic and political history. They form an inseparable part of that history and of its contemporary norms and institutions. Consequently, democracy is never just a theory or even a set of theories applied to or superimposed upon different countries, which thereby takes on "local color." On the one hand, each democratic country is historically, institutionally and demographically unique and therefore its codes and practices of democratic citizenship are also unique. On the other hand, the diversity of democratic institutions and their inextricable relations to specific national or ethnic contexts—a material and historical diversity that can never be adequately described by democratic theories—does not therefore invalidate a theoretical examination of paradigms of democracy.

An analysis and critique of democratic theories and institutions remains necessary because all democratic societies, no matter how distinct from one another and how internally complex, rely upon conceptual models, codes and commonplaces—whether in the form of nationalist or ethnic myths and ideologies, liberal/individualist promises of freedom and equal opportunity, or postulations of social equality and fraternity among men—in order to justify maintaining or changing their configurations of the socio-political order and their definitions of citizenship. In this more or less hidden and highly mediated fashion, Enlightenment theories still play a very important role in current democratic practices. They not only historically determine (in part) the nature and development of Western democratic institutions, but also function as part of the underlying codes that form our political assumptions, imaginary, institutions and the nature of our political dialogues.

By this I do not, of course, mean to suggest that politicians, when they promise to represent the "will of the people" at election time, are actually referring to or have even read Rousseau's formulation of the "general will." Rather, I argue that the vocabulary and concepts of Rousseau and other influential political philosophers have affected the way we think about and institutionalize democratic politics so profoundly that they find their way into our most immediate and commonplace assumptions concerning the nature and objectives of democratic societies. Similarly, Wollstonecraft's call for women's suffrage in the name of their similarity to men, or Olympe de Gouges's call for political parity between men and women based upon an argument of gender-based justice, all resurface in similar contemporary feminist proposals, even if those critiques and proposals are made in completely different historical contexts. Enlightenment concepts that outline the proper organization of democratic societies are so frequently invoked that they may seem self-justified and self-explanatory. This complacency concerning the political vocabulary, formulations, and normative frameworks of democratic citizenship is dangerous not only because it can camouflage gross social inequalities in the name of political justice and fraternity, as in the case of liberal individualism and fraternal republicanism. It is also problematic because it may fail to change the way we look at democratic citizenship, as in the case of feminist theories that do not examine, elaborate and explain the assumptions that support their alternative visions of democracy.

As suggested, one way to interrogate those assumptions is to return to some of their central, even if highly mediated, cultural influences in Enlightenment political theories and debates. I will use the four symptomatic passages cited at the beginning of this essay, all taken from Enlightenment political texts, as a means of illuminating some of the possibilities and impasses of contemporary democratic theories, especially with respect to correcting gender hierarchies. I will not describe either Enlightenment or the contemporary theories at any length. Instead, I will selectively analyze some of the assumptions and configurations they share, (without assuming that they share common historical or institutional formations) in order to introduce some of the contemporary debates and difficulties regarding the power asymmetries and sexism of Western democratic models of citizenship and their possible attenuation. For the most part, I will argue that Rousseau's and Wollstonecraft's theories can be, and in fact have been, used to buttress a liberal and (in practice) non-egalitarian model of democracy from, respectively, an anti-feminist and a proto-feminist angle. By contrast, de Gouges and Condorcet outline some of the principles which can serve more egalitarian and less sexist democratic movements.

More specifically, I will consider three kinds of democratic models: (1) the individualist/universalist and, relatedly, the republican/fraternal model of political impartiality proposed by Rousseau and reformulated by liberal democracies; (2) the model of sexual parity timidly sketched by Mary Wollstonecraft, radicalized by Olympe de Gouges and more systematically discussed by contemporary feminist political theorists, including Anne Phillips and Iris Marion Young; and (3) the model of proportional group-based representation hinted at by Condorcet's citation (though not defended in his work) and, once again, elaborated in a particularly compelling fashion by Iris Marion Young. In examining these three paradigms of democratic citizenship, my interrelated goals are to contribute to the already existing feminist critiques of liberal democracy and to defend what I call a "group-based and egalitarian," as opposed to a "individualist and hierarchical," model of democratic citizenship.

In endorsing political parity between men and women in government positions and other consecrated cultural and political functions, I will follow de Gouges's lead and distance my defense from what I view as its most perilous justification. That is, I will not rely upon "mirror-representation" paradigms which posit that social groups are so internally homogeneous, static, and clearly defined that any elected members from a given group will adequately represent the views, interests and beliefs of that group as a whole.[11] According to this logic, elected women can adequately represent all women; elected blacks can represent all blacks; elected gays and lesbians can represent all gays and lesbians, supposedly because all the members of these respective groups are necessarily essentially similar among themselves and essentially different from members of other groups. Equally dangerously, by the same logic members of each group have no affiliations and share nothing significant in common with members of other groups. Consequently, according to this sectarian model, the interactions among groups can be either neutral or antagonistic, but not positive and affiliatory.

This set of assumptions does not differ fundamentally from liberal individualist/universalist and communitarian/fraternal paradigms of political representation which take one group characteristic—"rationality," "masculinity," "fraternity," ethnic identity, etc.—and assume that this quality is so essential and common to all citizens worthy of political participation that any members elected among them will adequately represent the interests and opinions of the entire group. Analogously, mirror-representation theories take one group-based characteristic—for example, homosexuality in the case of gay and lesbian groups—as the essential characteristic which defines that group to the exclusion of other characteristics like gender, race, and class, which may actually play equally important roles in shaping the sociopolitical affiliations and antagonisms of members of that group and thus of the group itself. By defining group identity in this unitary and homogeneous fashion, liberal individualist/universalist and communitarian models of democratic citizenship leave little room for the antagonisms and multiple affiliations which, as discussed in the previous essays, characterize all group formations. The discussion in this essay therefore continues the trajectory of the other four essays by moving from abstract to increasingly pragmatic models and critiques of subject-citizenship and offers an open-ended articulation of some of the normative assumptions and political goals behind my former critique of the universal citizen-subject and defense of more egalitarian versions of democratic citizenship.

In the above citation, Rousseau outlines the notion of the abstract citizen-subject who lays aside his partial interests in order to participate in the concrete political process of voting and express the general will of the people. Rousseau claims, "It is important, then, in order to have a clear declaration of the general will, that there should be no partial association in the State, and that every citizen should express only his opinion." According to Rousseau, there are two principal political dangers.

First, the concrete individual could allow his personal background and biases to influence his otherwise impartial and universal political judgment, to be expressed by means of the vote. Second, Rousseau fears that even originally impartial individuals could join biased and self-interested groups that would distort their otherwise unselfish consideration of the general will.

As we can see, Rousseau's paradigm is simultaneously *individualist* and *collectivist*. It is individualist because its unit of citizenship is an abstract, rational yet sensitive individual who represents a universal type as opposed to an individuated or particular person. At the same time, Rousseau's unit of citizenship is fraternal/republican because it defines the political sphere in terms of a collectivity of abstract individuals who harmoniously express the general will of the nation as a whole. Consequently, Rousseau's formulations of the individuals and of the fraternal/republican order of the state are distinct, interdependent, and homologous. They are distinct because the individual and the collective are obviously different ontological categories, the sum total of individuals making up the group of male citizens, or otherwise stated, the fraternal republican order. They are interdependent because the republican community—"the body politic" or "the people"—could never exist without the individual citizens. Nor conversely, could the category of the individual citizen who is supposed to identify and express the "general will" of the community exist or have any qualities and functions without an understanding of the nature and organization of the republican community. Finally, they are homologous because both categories of citizenship—the male citizen-subject and the fraternal-republican community—rely upon identical political and epistemological processes. The individual and the community must follow a universalist and disinterested process of thought—the individual abstracted from his singularity, the community from its communitarian and sectarian interests—in order to purify itself/themselves from potentially dangerous partialities that would distort the general will.

As discussed earlier, the political model proposed by Rousseau is neither liberal nor democratic. In the *Social Contract*, Rousseau explicitly admits the hierarchical nature of his political community by claiming that "[t]aking the term in its strict sense, there never has existed, and never will exist, any true democracy. It is contrary to the *natural order* that the majority should govern and that the minority should be governed." (70) For Rousseau, the underlying principle of republican society is hierarchy, not equality. However, liberal/individualist theories that attempt to construct a democratic order tend to rely upon the three key assumptions (in milder versions) articulated by Rousseau's universalist republican ethics: (1) that the people of a nation are so similar that, under the proper conditions and following the correct procedures, each individual can identify and express the "general will" of the nation as the whole; (2) that this truth can be identified by all proper citizen-subjects only in isolation from interaction (be it antagonistic or affiliatory) with other (groups of) citizens; and (3) that the general will can only be identified once personal

Justice, Equality and Proportional Group Representation

desires, biases, histories, and interests are completely extricated from one's judgment (and, by extension, that this impartial judgment is possible and desirable to begin with). In the essay devoted to a critique of Rousseau's and Kant's universalizability principle, I have attempted to show that these principles are impossible, undesirable, and sustain a discriminatory and exclusionary politics that benefits privileged groups and continues to discriminate against disadvantaged groups, including women.

Moreover, as I have also previously suggested, Rousseau's "body politic" is a highly abstract and delimited entity rather than a concrete and inclusive political body. Not only is "the body politic" predicated upon abstract ideals (such as impartiality and the ability to discern the general will), but it also concretely excludes all human beings and social groups who are not ontologically, epistemologically, and politically defined as proper citizen-subjects. Since some human beings, such as women, are assumed to be essentially guided by subjective sentiments and desires rather than by the proper mixture of reason and emotion, they are deemed incapable of expressing the general will and are automatically excluded from political participation.

Superficially, we can accept Rousseau's claim that in his socio-political model, women are complementary to male citizens. However, this sexual complementarity does not imply a socio-political equality between women and men. Rousseau's version of strictly masculine citizenship constructs women's social inferiority. Consequently, we cannot charge Rousseau's paradigm with being gender-blind, as future (liberal/individualist) models of citizenship would be or at least claim to be. On the contrary, Rousseau's model of citizenship not only acknowledges sexual difference and the fact that people are divided by group-based inequalities and personal and communitarian interests, but also, generously enough, proposes a solution to these differences and potential divisions by excluding "other" groups from the political participation and representation granted to "republican" male citizen-subjects.

In some respects, Wollstonecraft and Condorcet employ political assumptions similar to those articulated by Rousseau. In the second quotation cited at the beginning of this essay, Wollstonecraft accepts the Enlightenment postulate of the male citizen-subject as the perfect norm and the female subject as the inferior and sometimes complementary exception. However, as we have seen, this kind of assumption does not lead her to conclude, along with her near contemporaries Rousseau, Kant, and Montesquieu, that women should therefore be excluded from citizenship. Adopting a strategy closer to Condorcet's, she believes in and charts the rational progress of both male and female subjects, or, more accurately, of the abstract individual and of human societies in general. For Wollstonecraft, mapping out this progress does not necessarily entail questioning most of the basic assumptions of liberal/individualist democracy. In stating, "Let women share the rights [of man] and she will emulate the virtues of man, for she must grow more perfect when emancipated, or justify the authority that chains such a weak being to her duty," Wollstonecraft seems to imply that if women, though naturally and/or culturally weaker and less rational than men, could be educated in the same rational fashion as men, then they, too, would be worthy of the political rights and responsibilities granted to men.

Consequently, adopting a set of assumptions which many identitarian liberal feminists who argue for complete gender-neutrality in laws and formulations of citizenship continue to propose today, Wollstonecraft defines political equality between women and men as a political identity of women with men. On the one hand, her paradigm challenges Rousseau's vision of complementary sexual difference by proposing that women could and should be educated to become more similar to men and that this education would enable women to become legal citizens along with men. On the other hand, the gender problematic she establishes remains enclosed within the terms that had defined a masculine paradigm of citizenship. First, she begins with a masculine ontological definition of citizenship by using the supposedly virile faculty of "Reason" as a basis for the kind of critical and impartial thinking necessary for the exercise of citizenship functions in the public sphere. She apologetically declares that,

> Yet, because I am a woman, I would not lead my readers to suppose that I mean violently to agitate the contested question respecting the equality or inferiority of sex; but as the subject lies in my way, and I cannot pass it over without subjecting the main tendency of my reasoning to misconstruction, I shall stop a moment to deliver, in a few words, my opinion. In the government of the physical world it is observable that the female in point of strength is, in general, inferior to the male. This is the law of nature; and it does not appear abrogated in favor of woman. A degree of physical superiority cannot, therefore, be denied—and it is a noble prerogative! But not content with this natural pre-eminence, men endeavor to sink us lower, merely to render us alluring objects for a moment; and women, intoxicated by the adoration which men, under the influence of their senses, pay them, do not seek to obtain a durable interest in their hearts, or to become the friends of the fellow creatures who find amusement in their society. (76)

Wollstoncraft assumes that "natural" or "biological" sexual difference renders women not simply physically weaker, but also more affected and constrained by their biological sexual natures and less rational than men. Thus she begins with the premise that women are *ontologically* weaker than men. Second (and relatedly), she also relies upon a masculinized *epistemology* by arguing that women could acquire the rational skills necessary for citizenship only if they were to be educated in the same fashion as men. She thus validates only a masculine definition of being and a masculinized process of attaining knowledge. The only thing she wishes to change—and this is a major, if difficult, shift—are the political implications of these ontological and epistemological codes and assumptions. However, Wollstonecraft's inability to question the cultural logic and premises that motivate discrimination against women renders her objectives of attenuating sexism much less effective

Justice, Equality and Proportional Group Representation

than, for example, de Gouges's more radical and critical evaluation of masculine laws and codes.

Wollstonecrafts's androcentric framework is inscribed in the very nature of her discourse. For example, it becomes immediately obvious that Wollstonecraft's tract, unlike de Gouges's, does not engage in a socio-political dialogue with both men and women. Men, and their understanding of social codes and citizenship, are the primary, if not the sole, interlocutors addressed by her text. In the introduction to *A Vindication of the Rights of Woman*, she claims, "I call with the firm tone of *humanity*; for my arguments, Sir, are dictated with a disinterested spirit—I plead for my sex—not for myself." (69) Moreover, while beginning her statement with the implication that she, as an individual woman, is making an argument or plea for human justice in general, she completes her phrase by claiming that she is speaking not as an individual, but in the name of a whole group—namely, for her sex, rather than for herself—and arguing for a gender-specific form of justice. The way she has set up the twin problematics of human versus gender-specific codes of justice and of individual-versus group-representation versions of citizenship leaves Wollstonecraft in a double-bind. Her acceptance of "human" (meaning masculine or gender-neutral) norms of justice as her basic normative framework undermines her later plea for sex-specific ethics. Similarly, her claim to impartiality on the basis of speaking for her sex rather than herself is completely unpersuasive given the fact that impartiality, at least as culturally defined by the discourses of male philosophers during the Enlightenment, implied distancing one's argument from both personal and group-based interests and affiliations. Wollstonecraft's effort to make a space for gender-specific laws within otherwise unaltered masculine codes of citizenship proves a very difficult and self-undermining task. In addition, Wollstonecraft's ontological and epistemological assumptions inflect—or are inflected by—her socio-political objectives.

It seems that Wollstonecraft is (rhetorically) less interested in ameliorating the status of women for women themselves, even though it is in their name that she claims to speak, as much as for the sake of men and for the good of a masculine society. She proposes that rational education and access to citizenship would better prepare Woman "to become the companion of man," so that she will not "stop the progress of knowledge and virtue; for truth must be common to all, or it will be inefficacious with respect to its influence on general practice." (70) Furthermore, this political "freedom [would] strengthen her reason till she comprehend her duty, and see in what manner it is connected to her real good." (70) Last but certainly not least, she argues, "If children are to be educated to understand the true principle of patriotism, their mother must be a patriot; and the love of mankind, from which an orderly train of virtues spring, can only be produced by considering the moral and civil interest of mankind; but the education and situation of woman, at present, shuts her out from such investigations."(70) In spite of itself, Wollstonecraft's theory of citizenship duplicates the division of spheres she attempts to partially dissolve. Her (re)formulation of citizenship employs already existing gender codes—of masculine rationality versus feminine frivolity, human/masculine-universal progress versus feminine contingency, civilized masculinity versus uneducated femininity, the masculine public sphere versus feminine maternity and domesticity—in order to argue for their subversion.

Hence, at the same time that it challenges masculinist definitions of the citizen-subject and of the public sphere, Wollstonecraft's paradigm of citizenship leaves intact three of its most basic assumptions which have supported, and continue to support, the (sometimes contradictory) logic and institutions of liberal democracies: (1) that women are biologically or ontologically less prepared for rational citizenship than men; (2) that women and men constitute two naturally and politically distinct and internally homogeneous groups (i.e., all men are similar among themselves, all women are similar among themselves and, moreover, these two gendered groups are socially and biologically complementary to each other); and (3) that in order to correct women's socio-political disadvantages in the public sphere—insofar as it is socially possible to compensate for women's natural weaknesses—women must be subject to the same laws and education that govern men and that are instituted by the men who have cultural and political power. These assumptions enclose Wollstonecraft's feminist propositions within self-defeating masculinist codes. Anne Phillips aptly encapsulates the feminist dilemma between upholding gender-blind policies that aspire to create women's equality *with men* and gender-specific policies that articulate women's differences *from men*, both of which take men as the comparative and sometimes regulative standard according to which to assess women:

> Strict equality legislation may abstract from the real conditions of women, giving them the formality of equal opportunity, but in practice leaving them stuck in a subordinate role. The alternative, however, is a risky business, for sex-specific legislation writes into our laws and practices that women are naturally different from men—which may confirm men as normal and ourselves in need of special help. For Eisenstein, the dilemma rests on the abstractions of the individual. The male has been the reference point in all our phallocentric discourses, with the supposedly gender-free language of individuals an increasingly threadbare disguise. . . . Our discussions of equality have always privileged this male body. . . . When men and women are treated the same, it means that women are treated as if they were men; when men and women are treated differently, the man is the norm, against which the woman is peculiar, lacking and different. Feminism has been endlessly locked into this equality/difference dichotomy—they are the only two choices yet neither will do.[12]

Wollstonecraft's political paradigm, like future feminist liberal models of citizenship, can be usefully described by means of the analogy of a competition between women and men. In this race men begin from a great advantage in at least three ways.

First, since men have more power and consecration than women, or, to use the same analogy, more training, more facilities, more coaches, and more fans, they start ahead. Consequently, despite the appearance of equality or of equal opportunity, which is deceptively suggested by the model of being evaluated by the same standards and of participating in the same competition, women and other historically disadvantaged groups begin from a starting point which is far behind privileged groups of men. Second, disadvantaged groups face barriers or hurdles (such as lack of economic support or outright discrimination) that privileged groups of men do not have to overcome. Third, men's strengths, in this case, rationality, universalist impartiality of judgment, and political acumen, determine the unquestioned criteria for winning the competition. Fourth, men are the judges in this unequal and unfair race because they disproportionately occupy the uppermost positions of power.

Nevertheless, despite men's comparative institutional advantages and women's comparative disadvantages and impediments, liberal political and economic theories, even those that ostensibly proclaim egalitarian ideals, mandate that both women and men must participate in this competition as if they began from equal starting points, as if they faced the same obstacles, and as if both sexes determined the standards and evaluated the performance of the competition. It should be noted that the same kind of logic applies to all kinds of competitions between socio-politically advantaged and disadvantaged groups. Tellingly, in today's political context (in the United States), it is conservative groups which most fervently uphold such (falsely) gender-neutral standards of justice and liberal/universalist definitions of subject-citizenship.

The third citation mentioned above, borrowed from Olympe de Gouges's *Declaration of the Rights of Woman and Female Citizen*, seems to be written in the same spirit as the citation from Wollstonecraft's *Vindication*, De Gouges proclaims,

> The mothers, daughters, and sisters, women representing the Nation, ask to be constituted as a National Assembly. Whereas ignorance, oblivion and contempt of the rights of women are the sole causes of public misfortune and of the corruption of governments, they have resolved to lay out in a solemn declaration, the natural, sacred and inalienable rights of woman, in order that this declaration, ever present before the members of the body social, be a constant reminder of their rights and duties. This in order that the acts of power by women, and those of power by men, may be at every moment comparable to the ends of any political institution and thereby all the more respected; and that the grievances of woman Citizens, henceforth founded on simple and incontestable circumstances, be ever turned toward upholding the Constitution and toward the welfare and happiness of all.

As the title of her tract indicates, de Gouges seems to desire to use the *Declaration of the Rights of Man*, even if partly in jest, as a model for her *Rights of Woman*. Furthermore, the use of "Woman" and "Man" in the singular initially indicates that in this text they are considered relatively abstract individuals rather than as internally diverse groups. Apparently, this formulation does not challenge one of the most basic premises of republican individualism, which conceptually and politically ignores differences within and among social groups.

Nevertheless, I would like to argue that, despite these initial appearances, de Gouges's work fundamentally challenges some of the republican assumptions that it seems to uphold. The very choice of setting up a *Declaration of the Rights of Woman* as opposed to either denying women political rights—like Rousseau, Montesquieu, and Kant—or of extending the *Rights of Man* to women—like Wollstonecraft—indicates that de Gouges is aware of women's separate social status and political disadvantages and wishes to amend those inequalities. Her formulation escapes in part the feminist dilemma we have alluded to earlier—judge women as either different and unequal or identical and unequal according to masculinist criteria—because she no longer employs masculine versions of citizenship as the norm which women must hopelessly strive to complement, differentiate themselves from, or approximate.

Correlatively, de Gouges does not rely upon conventional definitions of women or femininity and consequently does not set up a gynocentric model of citizenship that would neatly follow the division of spheres and define women's civic role as radically different from and complementary to that of male citizens. By disassembling the problematic of gender identity versus gender complementarity, she questions and redefines the conventional boundaries of sexual difference. Furthermore, although de Gouges emulates the masculine republican model and uses the term "Woman" in the singular, it is not at all clear from her statements that she assumes women to constitute a homogeneous group. Instead, she seems primarily concerned with empowering women on a par with men while at the same time acknowledging that both women and men form heterogeneous groups divided and united by many kinds of historical, ideological, and interpersonal affiliations.

Thus, although de Gouges's model of subject-citizenship is not gender-blind, as Rousseau's or as later liberal/universalist models would appear to be, it does not conform to gender stereotypes of sexual complementarity as republican models of citizenship tend to do. In fact, de Gouges *strategically* combines gender-neutral and gynocentric criteria in order to offset the entrenched phallocentrism of republican versions of citizenship. As Gayatri Spivak reminds us in *Inside the Teaching Machine*, a "strategy" is not a policy or rule that can be applied to every situation. It is an action which is devised and suited for a particular situation or set of circumstances. In those circumstances where she assesses that sexual difference is not relevant to particular social or political policies, de Gouges extends the Rights of Men—understood as basic human rights in a democratic society—to women. By contrast, in those circumstances in which she believes that gender does make a difference—and in fact tends to work to the socio-political advantage of men and to the disadvantage of women—de Gouges proposes gynocentric laws that can offset some of the deep-founded social prejudices and uneven power relations which work to systematically disadvantage women. As Spivak's description of strategy postulates, de Gouges does not exhaustively describe in advance which kinds of circumstances call for gynocentric laws and which call for gender-neutral laws, leaving these decisions up to historical (re)formulations. She does offer, however, some helpful indications which are applicable to her own historical context, namely eighteenth-century revolutionary France.

For example, she suggests that in sharing political and social power, gender should not make any difference in the sense of excluding or disadvantaging either men or women. Along with men, women "demandent d'être constituées en Assemblée nationale." These rights include gender-neutral rights such as social and political equality between all men and women, or the rights to "la liberté, la propriété, la sûreté, et surtout la résistance à l'oppression,"and new rights that attempt to establish the socio-economic equality of women with men like equal rights in sharing, inheriting and transmitting property, or, relatedly, equal shares in the "distribution of posts, employments, offices, dignities and industries," "in public administration, and in the determination of the rate, base, extent and term of the tax." (207–211)

Not shunning the realms of politics and law just because they had been codified as masculine (as her near-contemporaries, Madame de Roland and Madame de Staël, would do), de Gouges saw the necessity of targeting these domains precisely because they became so intrinsically masculinized during the eighteenth-century that they provided the most effective means of discriminating against women. Her decision to get women involved in masculinized domains resonates with Luce Irigaray's much later claim that sexual inequalities would be significantly ameliorated "by the recognition that different laws exist for each sex and that equivalent social status can only be established after these laws have been encoded by civil society's elected representatives."[13] Today, as in the eighteenth century, civil laws are rarely gender-blind. More often than not they endorse sexual stereotypes, especially when family roles and privileges are at stake. In the eighteenth century these stereotypes were employed to exclude women from legal and political rights while still making them subject to legal responsibilities—even more so than men—by strictly defining their duties to their spouses and children. Similarly, in the twentieth-century these stereotypes often reinforce women's "legal" right to be properly maternal or domestic, especially with regard to custody and "mommy-track" employment cases. By contrast to these separate and unequal gender laws, De Gouges's and Irigaray's calls for separate laws for women and men aim to protect the equal rights between women and men and thus to destabilize rather than reinforce gender stereotypes and hierarchies.

The kinds of changes in the legal framework endorsed by de Gouges presuppose a dramatic shift in the status and definition of the citizen-subject. First, whereas the individualist/universalist definitions of citizenship provided by Rousseau, Kant, Montesquieu and other political theorists began with the normative category of sameness, of judgement, reason, opinion, as the basis for the political structure of citizenship, de Gouges begins, like contemporary feminist critics, with the political and ontological category of difference as the basis of citizenship. According to de Gouges, sexual difference is one of the most basic ways in which people differ from one another: in their roles, habits, appearance, behavior and other important aspects of life. This difference has functioned to privilege men, under the false pretense that only they can represent universality, and to marginalize women. However, this difference, like other group-based differences, should be neither ignored nor essentialized. Opting for a middle ground between individualist universalism and group-based essentialism, de Gouges proposes that social differences must be acknowledged and used as a means of achieving sexual and socio-political equality. Such a formulation of citizenship anticipates Luce Irigaray's call for "laws that valorize difference. Not all subjects are the same, nor equal, and it wouldn't be right for them to be so. That's particularly true for the sexes. Therefore, it's important to understand and modify the instruments of society and culture that regulate subjective and objective rights. Social justice, and especially sexual justice, cannot be achieved without changing the laws of languages and the conceptions of truths and values structuring the social order."(*Je, tu, nous*, 22)

Like Irigaray, de Gouges maintains that women and men should have equal rights and power because that would be only fair and just. In making this claim, she does not start from a defensive position by attempting to persuade the audience of male representatives of the validity of her proposal on their terms and according to their gender-based assumptions. Instead, she turns the tables around and attacks their culturally accepted codes of sexual asymmetry: "O Man, are you capable of being just? . . . Tell me who has given you sovereign power to oppress my sex? Your force? Your talent? Behold the Creator in his wisdom; go through Nature in all her splendor (you seem to wish to approach her), and give me, if you dare, an example of such tyrannical dominion." (205) Ingeniously, de Gouges combines some of the deist and empiricist assumptions that were gaining popularity during the late eighteenth-century. However, unlike naturalists such as Buffon and La Mettrie, she employs empiricist arguments concerning the laws of nature and the behavior of animals in order to defend sexual equality, not to uphold sexual hierarchies.

In itself this signals a major paradigm shift. Anticipating aspects of constructionist feminist movements that would emerge two hundred years later, de Gouges interrogates and subverts the use of naturalist or biological discourses to buttress and justify social policies that produce sexual inequalities. On a meta-critical level, de Gouges's reinterpretation of naturalist discourse signals a feminist appropriation of representations of women, which have mostly been achieved by men in all cultural and social domains. Once again she anticipates critiques like those suggested by Luce Irigaray's claim that her work (*Speculum*) "cannot suggest getting the 'female body' to enter the male corpus, as the female body has always figured into the male corpus. . . . *Speculum* criticizes the exclusive right of the use(s), exchange(s), representation(s) of one sex by the other. [. . .] What this implies is that the female body is not to remain the object of men's discourse or their various arts but that it become the object of a female subjectivity experiencing and identifying itself."(*Je, tu, nous,* 59)

De Gouges's second major contribution to feminist critiques consists in proposing a coherent and, for her times, revolutionary theory of sexual parity. In her model of democracy, men and women would share economic, social, cultural, and political power both in the private and the public spheres. This understanding of democracy is so revolutionary that it has only recently begun to be debated and implemented in European countries (by means of voluntary political party quota systems) and in the United States (by means of government-mandated affirmative action programs). Third, and equally importantly, de Gouges treats sexual inequality as a systemic aspect of all areas of life, not just the realm of politics proper. This broad framework enables her to propose reforming society as a whole, rather than addressing local aspects of gender-based asymmetries while leaving sexual codes and assumptions otherwise intact. In this respect as well de Gouges's proposal is far ahead not only of her times, but also of ours. For instance, de Gouges does not simply demand that women obtain an equal right to vote, as will later nineteenth-century European and American suffragettes. She realizes that the right to vote is a necessary but minimal, and certainly insufficient, means of achieving sexual equality in culture and society as a whole. In the words of Anne Phillips,

> The inadequacy of the vote is not just that it occurs so infrequently and provides no substantial popular control; as important is its assumption that interests are pre-given and the way this works is to sustain the status quo. The social construction of femininity and masculinity is such that we cannot simply accept initial positions as expressions of people's interests and needs. . . . [Votes and opinions] should not be taken as the first and last word, for when gender so profoundly structures our sense of ourselves and our interests, these original positions are ambiguous and suspect. [. . .] What is important here is that liberal democracy as currently practiced makes it hard even to address this dilemma, for it recurrently returns us to the individual as the basic unit of political life, blocking serious consideration of the empowerment of disadvantaged groups.[14]

De Gouges's work foreshadows many of the political and normative claims raised by feminists today—ranging from the proposals of NOW in the United States to the arguments for political parity made by feminist movements in France and other European nations, and even to the more pragmatic aspects of Luce Irigaray's ethics of sexual difference. It also foreshadows some of their difficulties and dilemmas. De Gouges's insufficient elaboration and examination of the critical issues of group-based representation and group-based heterogeneity leave her theory, as well as current theories that employ similar arguments, subject to potentially insurmountable objections. For example, who are the elected female representatives going to be, in what ways are they going to be representative and of whom, and by what kinds of democratic political processes will their proportionate election be ensured?

If, even within the context of universal suffrage, women are perfectly content with their status as second-class or, at the very least, disadvantaged citizens and continue to vote along with men against their gender-based empowerment, then how can de Gouges's program of poltical parity be democratically defended and instituted? She claims to be pleading the cause of the mothers, sisters, daughters and female representatives of her nation. But in what way and by whom is she authorized to represent the opinions of all women? Assuming that most women would have considered her proposal both radical and undesirable, in what ways do her feminist critiques, though certainly not representative of her countrywomen's opinions, remain valid? It seems that the postulation of gender-based parity and group-based representation is only a beginning in the difficult process of correcting the systemic group-based disadvantages in a democratic, politically self-critical and responsible fashion.

On the other hand, democratic theorists must contend with the question of whether it is just or fair to have only a minority of privileged men occupy the uppermost positions of political and cultural power. The most frequent answer to this question is "yes," if those privileged men are legitimately and democratically voted into power. The alternative answer offered by feminist and civil-rights activists is "maybe," but we must re-examine some of the underlying structural and social reasons why only white men are voted into power. Feminist critics, especially those who support sexual parity, tend to make two kinds of arguments, normative and pragmatic, that challenge the position of those who consider white-male hegemony completely legitimate provided that it is consolidated through democratic means.

The pragmatic vein of the feminist critique demonstrates that because of the many impediments, including discrimination against women and minorities, less access to funding, social prejudices concerning the superiority of whites, women and minorities rarely even make it to the ballot-box, let alone to be considered for the upper levels of political power and representation. Hence, the main difficulty is not that women and minorities are voted out of power or that white men are necessarily preferred to other social groups. This is where the second, normative, argument comes in: this systemic discrimination against women and minorities is not just or appropriate in genuinely democratic societies. As Anne Phillips summarizes it, feminist calls for political and cultural parity rely on the following rationales:

> Part of it lies on a notion of basic justice, and fits within a broad sweep of arguments that challenges sexual segregation wherever it occurs. Just as it is unjust that women be cooks but not engineers, typists but not directors, so it is unjust that they should be excluded from the central activities in the political realm; indeed, given the overarching significance of politics, it is even more unfair that women should be kept out of this. . . . Sometimes the argument is that women would bring to politics a different set of values, experiences and expertise: that women would enrich our political life, usually in the direction of a more caring, compassionate society. A more radical version is that men and women are in conflict and that it is nonsense to see

women represented by men. The case for justice says nothing about what women will do if they get into politics, while the two further arguments imply that the content of politics will change. All unite in seeing a sexual disproportion between electors and elected as evidence that something is wrong. The striking homogeneity of our existing representatives is proof of this, since if there were no substantial differences between men and women, between black people and white, then those elected would undoubtedly be a more random sample from those they elect. Consistent underrepresentation of any social category already establishes that there is a problem. Such a marked variance from the population as a whole could never be an accidental result. Leaving aside as mere prejudice the notion that women are 'naturally' indifferent to politics, there must be something that prevents their involvement. The argument from justice then calls on us to eliminate or moderate whatever obstacles we find to women's participation, while the arguments of women's different values go one stage further. (*Prospects for Democracy*, 62–63)

According to this logic, the argument from fairness still supports gender-based parity, but the argument from a more fair and representative election process supports a model of proportional representation rather than only a gender-based parity model. Since even a parity system, where men and women evenly share political and maybe even cultural positions of power, does not guarantee a more sensitive response to all disadvantaged communities (because both male and female representatives are likely to belong to privileged groups), then members of other disadvantaged groups should also have a political voice that is secured by democratic structures and procedures. Once again, members of other disadvantaged groups will not necessarily consider the best interests of their communities. Nevertheless, they would be more likely to attempt to ascertain what those changing, contextual interests are and to support policies that would at least partly favor those interests, at the very least for the pragmatic reason that their own political status is dependent upon the disadvantaged group they are supposed to represent. Hence, the argument for proportional representation, which in the case of women implies political parity, need not rely upon reductive models of mirror-representation and group-based homogeneity.

Condorcet's words, which sound uncannily prophetic given today's political debates and difficulties, begin to address the problems of group-based representation in the public sphere(s). As it turns out, this citation does not capture the spirit of *A Sketch for a Historical Picture of the Progress of Human Mind*, which proposes a largely universalist and gender-neutral version of the citizen-subject and charts a linear and ethnocentric version of social progress. Nevertheless, this citation, atypical both of Condorcet's own writings and the political writing of his time, does reveal that other kinds of considerations unsettled universalist models of citizenship, during and especially following the Enlightenment. Condorcet claims,

We shall demonstrate not only that this principle of identity of interests, once made the basis of political rights, is a violation of the rights of those who are thereby debarred from them, but also that this identity ceases to exist once it gives rise to genuine inequality. We shall insist on this point because the fallacy involved in accepting this principle is the only one still likely to be dangerous, since it is the only one to which intelligent men are not yet wholly alive.

As we have seen in our previous analyses, both republican or individualist democratic theories and group-based mirror representation theories begin with the premise that individuals and groups are or should be homogeneous in their political interests and judgments. Thus, both kinds of theories, despite their diverging political models and goals, begin and end up with what Condorcet calls the "principle of identity of interests" and what current poststructuralist feminists call an "identity politics." Condorcet himself seems ambivalent on this issue. On the one hand, he argues that the identity-of-interests principle obscures group-based and individual social inequalities. On the other hand, he suggests that if everyone were socially equal, then the principle of identity of interests could work in a fair and democratic fashion. In either case, Condorcet acknowledges that given the fact that social inequalities undeniably exist, we cannot rely upon a political theory which acted as if they do not.

Raising similar arguments, feminist theorists argue against liberal paradigms, including the rationalist paradigm proposed by Habermas discussed earlier, that ask us to bracket social inequalities from democratic debates. How to argue for a better paradigm of democratic citizenship which does not propose either individualist or group-based identity of interests is perhaps the greatest political and ethical challenge currently confronted—unfortunately, most often deliberately ignored—by contemporary democratic societies. In conclusion, I would like to suggest a model of democratic citizenship that would be more egalitarian and just than the ones made possible by various applications of the universalizability principle.

First, the unit of citizenship would no longer be the abstract subject, as in Kant and Rousseau, or the concrete but unitary individual, as in classical liberalist versions of citizenship. Instead, citizenship would be organized around concrete group formations, of both privileged and disadvantaged groups, all of which would have a direct voice in public deliberations. In other words, the concept of citizenship would be based upon some kind of notion of proportional representation that would permit all citizens to have equal access to public decisions.

Second, these groups would not be confused with either aggregates or collectives organized around arbitrary principles like sharing the same first name or living on the same street, or with special-interest groups, which would imply an emphasis upon shared political goals and opinions. On the contrary, citizenship would be organized around a definition of the group that is neither arbitrary nor closed nor ideologically predetermined. My understanding of "groups" is shaped by the description offered by Iris Marion Young in *Justice and the Politics of Difference*.[15] According to Young, groups are structured around ascriptive qualities like class, gender, race, ethnicity. These ascriptive qualities not only determine the historical and ideological formations, affiliations

Justice, Equality and Proportional Group Representation

and divisions among people, but also the comparative disadvantages and privileges among and within given communities. Young defines a group as follows:

> A social group is a collective of persons differentiated from at least one other group by cultural forms, practices, or way of life. Members of a group have a specific affinity with one another because of their similar experience or way of life, which prompts them to associate with one another rather than with those not identified with the group. . . . Groups are an expression of social relations; a group exists only in the encounters and interaction between social collectivities that experience some differences in their way of life and forms of association, even if they also regard themselves as belonging to the same society. (43)

According to this definition, the members of a group such as women are recognized as always socially and politically diverse and overdetermined. In the context of democratic public forums, this pattern of shared and diverging interests within each group would discourage the formulation of dogmatic and unitary ideologies and would enable each group to form affiliations with other groups.

A notion of citizenship organized around ascriptive group-formations would not be a strictly divisive institution and in fact would encourage people to find some common ground in specific contexts and to formulate some set democratic rules that could enable them to articulate both their agreements and their disagreements in a "rational" fashion. In this kind of democratic community, consensus, understood as an application of the universalizability principle, would be necessary for establishing the constantly negotiated legal and normative framework of a democratic society, but not in the sense of mandating agreement concerning either the abstract public good, as for Kant and Rousseau, or more specific and concrete issues, as for Habermas. A group-based understanding of democratic citizenship would permit the continual interweaving of the social interests of various political and social communities not in terms of shared identity or common principles, but, to use Wittgenstein's helpful formulation, "in a complicated network of similarities overlapping and criss-crossing: sometimes overall similarities, sometimes similarities of detail," which make up the pattern of our socio-political "family resemblances."[16]

NOTES

1 Jean-Jacques Rousseau, *The Social Contract*. New York: Washington Square Press, 1974, 31.

2 Mary Wollstonecraft, *A Vindication of the Rights of Woman*, edited by Janet Todd. Buffalo: University of Toronto Press, 1993, 295.

3 Olympe de Gouges, *Déclaration des Droits de la Femme et de la Citoyenne*. Paris: Côté-femmes, 1993, 206.

4 Antoine-Nicolas de Condorcet, *Sketch for a Historical Picture of the Progress of Human Mind*, trans. June Barraclough. New York, Noonday Press, 145.

5 "Liberal Democracy and the Limits of Democratization," *Prospects for Democracy*, edited by David Held. Palo Alto, CA: Stanford Universtiy Press, 1993, 55.

6 "Liberal Socialism and Pluralism: Which Citizenship?" in *Principled Positions*. London: Lawrence and Wishart, 1993, 80–84.

7 In *Muse de la Raison*, Geneviève Fraisse engages in a close symptomatic analysis of the Condorcet-Wollstonecraft poles of the masculine-neutral and sexually discriminatory formulations of citizenship which were proposed and enacted during the French Revolution. Paris: Editions Alinéa, 1989.

8 In her analysis of Wollstonecraft's writing, Zillah Eisenstein, in *The Radical Future of Liberal Feminism*, argues that Wollstonecraft's definitions of citizenship for women are contradictory. On the one hand, Wollstonecraft defines women's citizenship along the same lines as the rationalist citizenship in the public sphere that was being extended to men. On the other hand, she retains the gendered division of labor and relegates women to the private sphere as rational wives and mothers. I believe that this dual version of female citizenship is not so much contradictory as complementary. According to Wollstonecraft, both men and women are considered capable of being rational political participants, although men have a social and perhaps even a natural advantage. Thus, *a priori*, the male is the norm which the woman can strive to approximate up to a point. However, the fact that women can be rational does not imply, for Wollstonecraft, that they are therefore identical to men. Quite the contrary, she repeatedly criticizes masculine women and argues that women should be both rational and domestic. In other words, her vision is not one of cultural androgyny, but of a cultural complementarity where masculinity remains defined as rational and femininity is redefined as not only domestic but also rational. Her gender codes maintain both sexual complementarity and men's normative and superior social status.

9 Christine Planté discusses this feminist debate and its implications in detail in her article "Questions de différences," *Féminisme au présent, Supplément futur antérieur*. Paris: L'Harmattan, 1993.

10 *Feminist Studies* 14, no. 1, Spring 1988.

11 I should note, however, that I believe this justification is employed mostly as a "strawman" argument by those who want to dismiss feminist critiques by distorting them beyond validity or recognition, rather than by feminists themselves.

12 *Engendering Democracy*. College Station: The Pennsylvania State University Press, 1991, 37.

13 *Je, tu, nous: Toward a Culture of Difference*, trans. Alison Martin. New York: Routledge, 1993, 86.

14 "Must Feminists Give up on Liberal Democracy?" in *Prospects for Democracy*, 94–107.

15 *Justice and the Politics of Difference*. Princeton: Princeton Universtiy Press, 1990."

16 Ludwig Wittgenstein, *Philosophical Investigations*. London: Basil Blackwell, 1958.

BIBLIOGRAPHY

Aristotle, *The Oxford Translation of Aristotle*, ed. W. D. Ross. Oxford: Clarendon Press, 1912.

Armstrong, Nancy, *Desire and Domestic Fiction*. London: Oxford University Press, 1986.

Bakhtin, Mikhail, *The Dialogical Principle*, trans. Wlad Godzich. Minneapolis: University of Minnesota Press, 1984.

Bauman, Zygmunt, *Postmodern Ethics*, London: Blackwell, 1993.

Bell, David, *Circumstances: Chance in the Literary Text*. Nebraska: University of Nebraska Press, 1993.

Bourdieu, Pierre, *Distinction: A Social Critique of the Judgment of Taste*, trans. Richard Nice. Cambridge: Harvard University Press, 1984.

———, *The Field of Cultural Production*, ed. Randal Johnson. New York: Columbia University Press, 1993.

———, Pierre, *The Logic of Practice*, trans. Richard Nice. Palo Alto, California: Stanford University Press, 1990.

———, *Outline of a Theory of Practice*, trans. Richard Nice. Cambridge: Cambridge University Press, 1977.

Buber, Martin, *I and Thou*, trans. Ronald Gregor Smith. New York: Macmillan, 1958.

Butler, Judith and Joan W. Scott, eds., *Feminists Theorize the Political*. New York: Routledge, 1992.

————, *Bodies that Matter: On the Discursive Limits of "Sex."* New York: Routledge, 1993.

————, *Gender Trouble*. New York: Routledge, 1988.

Condorcet, Antoine-Nicolas de, *Sketch for a Historical Picture of the Progress of Human Mind*, trans. June Barraclough. New York, Noonday Press.

Derrida, Jacques, *Dissemination*, trans. Barbara Johnson. Chicago: University of Chicago Press, 1981.

————, *Of Grammatology*, trans. Gayatri Chakravorty Spivak. Baltimore: Johns Hopkins University Press, 1977.

Diderot, Denis, *Additions à la lettre sur les aveugles*. Paris: GF-Flammarion, 1972.

————, *Le Neveu de Rameau*. Paris: GF-Flammarion, 1991.

————, *La Religieuse*. Paris: GF-Flammarion, 1991.

Eisenstein, Zillah, *The Radical Future of Liberal Feminism*. Boston: Northeastern University Press, 1993.

Felski, Rita, *Beyond Feminist Aesthetics: Feminist Literature and Social Change*. Cambridge: Harvard University Press, 1989.

Flax, Jane, *Disputed Subjects: Essays on psychoanalysis, politics and philosophy*. New York: Routledge, 1993.

Fraisse, Geneviève, *Muse de la Raison*. Paris: Editions Alinéa, 1989.

Fraisse, Robert, "Pour une politique des sujets singuliers," in *Penser le Sujet: Autour d'Alain Touraine, Colloque de Cerisy*, ed. François Dubet and Michel Wieviorka. Paris: Fayard, 1995.

Fraser, Nancy, *Unruly Practices: Power, Discourse and Gender in Contemporary Social Theory*. Minneapolis: University of Minnesota Press, 1989.

Fuss, Diana, *Essentially Speaking: Feminism, Nature, and Difference*. New York: Routledge, 1989.

Giddens, Anthony, *Capitalism and Modern Social Theory*. London: Cambridge University Press, 1971.

Godineau, Dominique, *A History of Women in the West*, vol. IV, ed. Michelle Perrot and Geneviève Fraisse. Harvard: Harvard University Press, 1993.

Gouges, Olympe de, *Dèclaration des Droits de la Femme et de la Citoyenne*. Paris: Côté-femmes, 1993.

Goux , Jean-Joseph, *Symbolic Economies*, trans. Jennifer Gage. Ithaca: Cornell University Press, 1988.

Habermas, Jürgen, *Moral Consciousness and Communicative Action*. Cambridge: The MIT Press, 1991.

Held, David, "Liberal Democracy and the Limits of Democratization," in *Prospects for Democracy*, ed. David Held. Stanford: Stanford University Press, 1993.

Hunt, Lynn, *The Family Romance of the French Revolution*. Berkeley: University of California Press, 1992.

Irigaray, Luce, "Is the Subject of Science Sexed?" in *Feminism and Science*, ed. Nancy Tuana. Bloomington: Indiana University Press, 1989.

————, *J'aime à toi*, (I Love to You), trans. Alison Martin. New York: Routledge, 1995.

————, *Je, tu, nous: Toward a Culture of Difference*, trans. Alison Martin. New York: Routledge, 1993.

Kant, Immanuel, *Critique of Judgment, Philosophical Writings*, ed. Ernst Behler. New York: Continuum, The German Library, 1986.

————, *Groundwork of the Metaphysics of Morals*, trans. H. J. Paton. New York: Harper Torchbooks, 1948.

——, *Observations on the Feeling of the Beautiful and Sublime*, trans. John T. Goldthwait. Berkeley: University of California Press, 1960.

Kemp, Sandra and Paolo Bono, eds., *The Lonely Mirror: Italian Perspectives on Feminist Theory*. New York: Routledge, 1993.

Lyotard, Jean-François, *The Postmodern Condition: A Report on Knowledge*. Manchester: Manchester University Press, 1986.

Mouffe, Chantal, "Liberal Socialism and Pluralism: Which Citizenship?" in *Principled Positions*. London: Lawrence and Wishart, 1993.

Phillips, Anne, *Engendering Democracy*. College Station: The Pennsylvania State University Press, 1991.

——, "Must Feminists Give up on Liberal Democracy?" in *Prospects for Democracy*, ed. David Held. Palo Alto: Stanford University Press, 1993.

Planté, Christine, "Questions de différences," in *Féminisme au présent, Supplément futur antérieur*. L'Harmattan: Paris, 1993.

Pollock, Griselda, *Vision and Difference: Femininity, Feminism and the Histories of Art*. London: Routledge, 1988.

Rabinow, Paul, ed., *The Foucault Reader*. New York: Pantheon, 1984.

Rooney, Ellen, *Seductive Reasoning*. Ithaca: Cornell University Press, 1989.

Rousseau, Jean-Jacques, *Confessions*. Paris: GF Flammarion, 1987.

——, *The Social Contract and Discourses*, trans. by G. D. H. Cole. London: Everyman, 1973.

——, *The Social Contract*. New York: Washington Square Press, 1974.

Scott, Joan, "Deconstructing equality-versus-difference: or, the uses of poststructuralist theory for feminism," *Feminist Studies*, 14, no. 1, Spring 1988.

Sedgwick, Eve, "Adam Bede and Henry Esmond: Homosocial Desire and the Historicity of the Female," in *The New Historicism Reader*, ed. H. Avram Veeser. New York: Routledge, 1994.

Weil, Kari, *Androgyny and the Denial of Difference*. Charlottesville: University of Virginia Press, 1992.

Wolff, Janet, *The Social Production of Art*. New York: New York University Press, 1981.

Wollstonecraft, Mary, *A Vindication of the Rights of Woman*, ed. Janet Todd. Buffalo: University of Toronto Press, 1993.

Young, Iris Marion, *Justice and the Politics of Difference*. Princeton: Princeton University Press, 1990.

INDEX

Buber, Martin, 29
Butler, Judith: on "agreement," 54;
  on coalition, 57–58; in consideration of
  Habermas, 4–5, 42, 54; on knowledge, 42;
  on performance of gender roles, 17–18;
  on universality, 26–27, 34

C

"catagorical imperative," 35
censorship, 62–63
citizenship: as camouflage for social
  inequality, 82; conceptions of, 76–97;
  group-based, 5, 82–83, 94–97; individualist, 77, 82–85, 91–92, 94–95, 96; masculinist definitons of, 88; republican-
  communitarian, 78–79, 82–85; and
  subjecthood, 2–5, 83–84, 85, 88–89,
  95–97; sexual parity model, 82, 85–94
civil rights theorists, 76, 94
class, gender, and race in subject-positions,
  30–31
Condorcet, Antoine-Nicolas de, 78–80, 82,
  85, 95–96
Confessions (Rousseau), 19–20
consensus, 39–40, 54, 97
Contemporary French Civilization, 62
contractarian ethics, 34–39, 60
copula, the, 24, 28
Criticism and Ideology, The Function of Criticism
  (Eagleton), 50
cultural capital, 69

D

Declaration des Droits de l'Homme, 79, 90
Declaration of the Rights of Woman and Female
  Citizen (de Gouges), 89–90
"Deconstructing equality-versus-
  difference" (Scott), 80
Democratic and Republican parties, U.S., 77
democratic theories, contemporary, 5,
  75–76, 94–97
Derrida, Jacques: on mimetic theory, 65;
  on Rousseau, 13; on the supplément, 20–21
Descartes, René, 14–15, 55

dialogic subjectivity, 29–30
Diderot, Denis: dissimulation in, 8–9;
  on gendered subjectivities, 14–21;
  vs. Rousseau, 14, 21
difference: and aestheics, 63–74; and citizenship, 75–97; postmodern emphasis on, 3;
  in public sphere, 49–60; relativization of,
  4; sexual, 22–31, 86–87, 90–94
Discipline and Punish (Foucault), 18–19, 20–21
Discourse on the Origin of Inequality (Rousseau),
  12
Disputed Subjects (Flax), 44–45
dissimulation and republican order, 8–21
"Double Session, The" (Derrida), 65

E

Eagleton, Terry, 50
economic reductionism in aesthetics, 70–71
economies, masculine vs. feminine, 45–46
Eley, Geoff, 51–52
Elizabeth, Princess of Bohemia, 14
Equal Rights Amendment, 81

F

Felski, Rita, 72
femininity: production of, 19–20;
  representations of, 67
Flax, Jane, 43, 44–45, 57–58
Foucault, Michel: on the Panopticon, 18–19,
  20–21; on the universal subject, 2
Fraisse, Geneviève, 79
Fraisse, Robert, 3
Fraser, Nancy: on Habermas, 4–5, 41, 44,
  49–60; on public sphere, 44, 49–54,
  56–57, 59–60; on principle of universal-
  izability, 34, 41, 44, 49–60
French Enlightenment, the, 8–21, 76, 78–79
French Revolution: in history of democracy,
  75, 78, 79–80, 81–82; women's role in, 10
Fuss, Diana, 27

G

gendered intersubjectivity, 4
Gender Trouble (Butler), 17–18, 54